To Thaxter,

I know you love
the Boston Pops on
I'm giving you this
book Christmas 1983. READ
and Enjoy.

Love ya Daddy

Love,
Anne

Arthur Fiedler
and the
Boston Pops

Books by Harry Ellis Dickson

GENTLEMEN, MORE DOLCE PLEASE!
*An Irreverent Memoir of Thirty-five Years
in the Boston Symphony Orchestra*

ARTHUR FIEDLER AND THE BOSTON POPS

HARRY ELLIS DICKSON

Arthur Fiedler
and the
Boston Pops

An Irreverent Memoir

Prologue by
Ellen Bottomley Fiedler

Epilogue by
John Williams

Illustrated with Photographs

HOUGHTON MIFFLIN COMPANY BOSTON
1981

Library of Congress Cataloging in Publication Data
Dickson, Harry Ellis.
Arthur Fiedler and the Boston Pops.
1. Fiedler, Arthur, 1894–1979. 2. Boston Pops Orchestra. I. Title.
ML422.F53D5   785'.092'4 [B]   81-193
ISBN 0-395-30524-1   AACR2

Printed in the United States of America

P 10 9 8 7 6 5 4 3 2 1

The endpaper photograph is from the Boston Symphony Orchestra Archives.

To the memory of my wife

Acknowledgments

IF I HAD TO MAKE A LIVING AT WRITING I am sure I would starve to death, for I am a musician who is more comfortable with notes than with words. I want to thank so many people who have helped me to create words without music about a man who was a visible legend.

If this book causes me no trouble I am indebted first to Paul Conway, who told me I had to do it; then to my old friend, David Manning White, for his advice and encouragement; to my new friend, Michael Kaplan, for his untiring research and for uncovering things about A. F. even I didn't know; to Bruce MacPherson, for his friendly and professional advice; to David Mugar, Bill Cosel, and Bill Shisler for remembering things I had forgotten; to Carol Green and Emily Weingarth, Arthur's loyal and lovable secretaries for many years; to John Cronin of the Boston *Herald* and his associates for being the gentlemen they are for their patience in helping us relive the past with Mr. Pops; likewise to all my friends of the Boston *Globe*; to our new conductor, John Williams, for taking the time to write an epilogue; to his secretary and my helper, Nancy Clough, for her assistance in the preparation of my manuscript; to my long-suffering colleagues in the Boston Pops with whom I experienced the same love-hate relationship not only toward Arthur but toward all conductors; to Ellen Fiedler for her bubbly good humor and genuine candor; and finally, to my children, Kitty and Jinny, who, as their mother would have done, advised against some of the things that I said anyway.

Contents

Illustrations

(following page 78)

Arthur at the wheel of his fire engine
Photo courtesy of Boston Herald American

Danny Kaye and the author
Boston Symphony Orchestra Archives

Arthur and his Dalmatian

Mayor Kevin White with Arthur
and Seiji Ozawa, conductor of the BSO
Photo courtesy of Boston Herald American

Maestro Fiedler
William Shisler, Boston

Arthur with Joan Kennedy
Boston Symphony Orchestra Archives

Arthur and Ellen with Ray Bolger
Boston Symphony Orchestra Archives

Arthur with young ballerinas
Photo courtesy of Boston Herald American

An audience view of Arthur

An eightieth birthday celebration
Photo courtesy of Boston Herald American

Crowds gathering for the Bicentennial Concert
on the Esplanade, July 4, 1976
David Mugar

Arthur in a relaxed moment
William Shisler, Boston

Annual Pops Christmas concert
Photo courtesy of Boston Herald American

Listening to playbacks from a recording session
Copyright © 1978 Boyd Estus

Ellen Fiedler during a performance
of Copland's *Lincoln Portrait*
Photo courtesy of Boston Herald American

Arthur as he welcomed the Boston
Symphony Orchestra's return from China
Wide World Photos

Prologue

BY ELLEN BOTTOMLEY FIEDLER

SINCE THE AGE OF SEVEN, when I first met Arthur Fiedler, I have been madly in love with this man. I was among the very few who knew the Arthur that lived inside his public image, who caught a glimpse of what made this extraordinary man tick. For thirty-seven years I was married to him. I adored him, but it wasn't easy. He was impenetrable, a curmudgeon, often a great burden to me, but he never ceased to fascinate me. He had an aura — call it a charisma — that often amazed me, and thrilled me just as it did his audience. The Arthur I knew could be very cold. The Arthur I knew also shared some of his warmest, most private moments with me, and I am grateful to God that I was able to bring those moments out in him.

Harry knew both sides of Arthur, and he was not in awe of him. He saw Arthur's weaknesses — and his pretensions — probably better than anyone else. Harry remembers him as he was, crusty and difficult; but he remembers him with affection, admiration, and humor.

Overture

When Arthur Fiedler died on July 10, 1979, an incredible life came to an end — a life of personal triumph, controversy, and sheer will. It had never occurred to him that he should be grateful for his success, or that he owed anybody anything. My own association with him over the years was a love-hate relationship. I admired his ability and envied his accomplishments, even though he could not bring himself to let me like him.

The few times when I voiced my admiration his reaction was one of cynicism and disbelief. He neither needed nor expected my compliments. Toward the end of his life, when I spent a great deal of time with him — in the hospital and at home — he appeared to soften somewhat, but he still could not allow himself to accept me, or anyone else, as a close friend. Once, when he got up from his sick bed to escort me to the door to say good-bye, he almost put his arm on my shoulder, but he instinctively withdrew it. He simply could not bring himself to display any feelings of intimacy. It was then that I began to feel a deep sense of compassion and pity for this unusual man. This book is a release of my own personal feelings toward a man who was so much a part of my life and yet remained so distant. I have tried to describe Arthur Fiedler as he was, not as the public knew him.

Someone once said that to be great is to be misunderstood. Like Leonard Bernstein, also a product of the Boston Symphony Orchestra, Arthur's personality extended in many directions. Although his admirers were legion, he also had many detractors. Still, everything he did was convincing and vital. Over three hundred and seventy-five fire departments throughout the world made him an honorary chief. He was fascinated by violence, yet I have neither witnessed nor heard of a single incident where Arthur was physically violent himself. Although Arthur surrounded himself with people, he had no entourage and was a stranger to his own children. He was a good musician, but felt professionally threatened at every stage of his life. He was a traditionalist, conducting the masters exactly as the music had been written. Yet he was an iconoclast, advertising himself as a people's maestro — one who enjoyed exploiting the mundane and being part of boyish pranks on stage. He was an opportunist, but never once asked the symphony Trustees for an increase in salary. Arthur was, I believe, neither black nor white, but simply an indefinable shade of gray that often contrasted sharply to his own environment but somehow harmoniously blended with the image the public created of him.

I considered my ambivalent feelings at Arthur's death. I felt frustrated that I could not reach within myself to experience a number of warm recollections. He was not an outwardly warm, kind, or loving person. Whatever I shared with him was at arm's length, although as his life neared its end he mellowed a bit. I mourned the loss of a man who had given so much pleasure to millions of people, most of whom he had never met. For sixty-four years, first as a member of the Boston Symphony Orchestra, then as conductor of the Pops, Arthur's lifelong commitment to his craft established him as a part of Boston's history.

You are about to read an array of stories about Arthur. Some will portray a rather disagreeable, exasperating man. Paradoxically, others will show him to be kind, witty, dedicated, and admirable. I have tried to tell Arthur Fiedler's story as completely as possible. Of course it isn't truly complete, but I think most of his many sides are revealed in this book.

I do believe Arthur's story is one that should be told. Arthur belonged to a small group of popular music stars with an extraordinary mass appeal. He attracted audiences on a grand scale, comparable in numbers and faithfulness to fans of Bing Crosby, Frank Sinatra, or the Beatles. Often I wondered, through the years with Arthur, how the public could so ceaselessly love a man like him. I realize now it was more than his showmanship, more than the music. Arthur's image was lovable; he had a wolfishness about him, but it was a vulnerable wolfishness. Beyond that, little else mattered to the public about his private life. His eccentricities merely added to the fun. Arthur did not put himself on a pedestal. He was the people's conductor, and everyone could identify with him.

I have tried to tell the truth about a remarkably simple, deceptively complex human being — a man who achieved worldwide success, who had everything, and yet had nothing. If the world gained something from Arthur Fiedler he, himself, showed no personal joy in bringing it to them.

When, on the day of his death, I conducted the Pops in his memory, we closed the program with a quiet rendition of "The Stars and Stripes Forever." I gave the downbeat and left the stage as the orchestra played on, a riderless horse leading the final parade.

Prelude to the Pops

O<small>N THE HOT, BRIGHT AFTERNOON</small> of July 24, 1979, a
select group gathered inside the Harvard University Memorial Church to attend a Service of Thanksgiving for the Life of
Arthur Fiedler. Arthur had died two weeks before, and most of us
were not yet fully adjusted to his absence. Inside, I saw men and
women I had known for years whose faces were covered with
tears, together now in memory of all the times they had delighted
in Arthur's company. Outside, hundreds of people lounged on
the Yard, listening to the music and speeches from loud-speakers
set across the front of the church. Many of them did not even
know they were at a memorial service. This was an attraction for
them, a social event, much like a Boston Pops Concert. A small
orchestra of twenty musicians, only two of them from the Boston
Pops Orchestra, provided the music, and Berj Zamkochian was
the organist. By the time Maestro Seiji Ozawa began delivering
the first eulogy, it was obvious to all that this was a solemn, extremely heartfelt occasion. Everyone was silent as a distraught
Ozawa delivered in his broken English this deeply moving tribute:

After I heard that immortal music, as a musician . . . I have nothing
to say — to you, Ellen — but . . . you wanted me to speak here, so I

will. I think this must be a celebration, I know that; but it's very difficult for me, for you . . . he was like a father to me, he was a great friend to me, and I know he was a great friend for all of us . . . but for me especially. I grew up around the Boston Symphony, Tanglewood, so Arthur was there all the time. After I moved to Boston he was more close to me and we became very good friends. Sometimes he was stubborn, sometimes he was a sweet man, sometimes he was difficult, sometimes he was a very easy man, and an easy colleague. And I learned what is Tanqueray gin; I never tasted it until that moment and we enjoyed it. I think he enjoyed my little kids when we visited him when we'd get together at home and then the little game that started on. We have a mutual friend, Paul Kehayias. He's an usher today. He's the Boston Symphony's official driver — for him, for me, for guest conductors. At the beginning when we were shy, we — Arthur and I — used Paul's mouth so that when I felt Arthur was working too hard, I used to ask Paul to tell him "too much work, slow down, Arthur," and he did . . . I must also make very clear that many, many people became music lovers because of Arthur, not only in the United States but . . . in Asia and also Europe. To do that, to make people music lovers, was really genius and very unique. And also I know that Arthur made very special ties in this city, this area, the Boston area, between people and music, and this is very unique and we must keep going . . . And I'm very happy that the last six or seven years since I've been working for the Boston Symphony, I have worked together with Arthur. That was a very unique experience, too. I lost, I must say, a great friend and also he was a little bit like a father to me; and he's a spirit, I know for Boston people . . . I know he will stay with us a long, long time . . . he'd want it to be that way and we want him to be that way . . .

In preparing the book I have realized that I have no actual first-hand knowledge of Arthur's early years, but through conversations with him and his family I have tried to put the pieces together.

Arthur was particularly irked by the continual confusion over the years as to his ancestry. Who was his father? Was it Max Fiedler, Emanuel, Gustave, Bernard, or William Max? To settle the question, Arthur invited William Max Fiedler, a California music teacher, to guest conduct the Boston Pops. They would play a piece written by William's father, Max, when he was conducting the 1908 Boston Symphony Orchestra, which included Emanuel. One Boston music critic still had no understanding of the Fiedler relationship even after the publicity department at Symphony Hall drew up a genealogy chart. Finally, out of desperation and a sense of historical reference, Arthur called a Symphony Hall press conference prior to William Max Fiedler's guest conducting appearance and set straight the Fiedler relationships.

"The Max Fiedlers," Arthur pointed out, "are of German descent and my family is Austrian. The fact that so many Fiedlers have been connected with the Boston Symphony Orchestra has led a great many people to assume that we are all related. We all have the same name, which, of course, means 'fiddler.' The name fits my side of the family quite well — perfectly, in fact. My father, Emanuel, was a Boston Symphony violinist for twenty-five years. He was also a member of the Adamowski and Kneisel quartets. My uncles Bernard and Gustave Fiedler, my father's two brothers, were also violinists with the Boston Symphony. I also have a cousin, Joe Zimbler, who played with the BSO, but since we don't have the same last name (he was from Pilsen, Czechoslovakia, and we were from Vienna, Austria), I know there won't be any additional confusion."

Beginning with his great-grandfather, four generations were all violinists. Arthur's father was a graduate of the Vienna Conservatory of Music at twenty-two, a classmate of Fritz Kreisler, and a Gold Medal violinist. Born in the tiny hamlet of Sambor, Austria, Emanuel had considered a concert career very early in life. Employment as a musician was tenuous at best, and the pay was ridiculously low except for those few who had become virtuosos at a young age.

After his engagement to Johanna Bernfeld, Emanuel seriously considered another field of endeavor, but his old Viennese music teacher, Wilhelm Gericke, had become the Boston Symphony Orchestra's second conductor, and offered Emanuel a permanent violinist's chair.

At twenty-six and still single, Emanuel came to the United States and joined the Boston Symphony Orchestra in the fall of 1885. Promising Johanna that the moment he settled in America he would return to Vienna to marry her, he found a tiny flat on Columbus Avenue in Boston shortly after the close of the first season of the Promenade Concerts, later to become known as the Pops.

Three years passed before Emanuel could afford to return to Vienna. By that time over four hundred love letters had been exchanged between him and Johanna. They were married in 1888, honeymooned along the way to Bremerhaven, Germany, and took the first available boat to Boston, arriving in America in time for the opening of the Boston Symphony Orchestra's fall season. They settled in a small second-floor Columbus Avenue apartment less than two blocks from Emanuel's old room, and soon discovered that Johanna was pregnant. Uncomfortable with the thought of having a baby so far away from friends and family, in the spring of 1890 Johanna returned to Vienna, where Fredericka was born. Fritzie or Ricka, as she was alternately called through her life, arrived in Boston with her mother during the summer of 1891. A year later, her sister Elsa was born in Boston in a home delivery, as was the custom of the day. By now, the small apartment on Columbus Avenue was becoming impossibly cramped, and larger accommodations were obviously in order. But it was not until the summer of 1894 that they finally moved to a middle-class apartment-hotel on Sterling Street in the South End of Boston. Known as Madison Park, it was the home of many of Emanuel's colleagues and only a short walk to the Music Hall, where the Boston Symphony played.

During the interim period between Emanuel's arrival in America and Johanna's third pregnancy, Emanuel had firmly established himself in Boston. In the decade that had passed, he had become a well-known member of the Boston Symphony Orchestra, and soon after became second violinist with the Kneisel Quartet, an internationally famous chamber music ensemble composed exclusively of BSO musicians. Emanuel was highly touted as a violin teacher, and many of his students later joined the Boston Symphony, several remaining throughout their lifetimes. He enjoyed a rare relationship with Arthur Nikisch, the Hungarian-born, Vienna-educated conductor of the Boston Symphony Orchestra from 1889 to 1893; and when a son was born to Johanna and Emanuel on December 17, 1894, they named him Arthur, in honor of Nikisch. During a customary family summer vacation in Austria, Rosa, their last child, was born in 1897 at her maternal grandmother's home.

European to the core, Emanuel loved the Continental lifestyle and never became an American citizen. He insisted that all his children speak German rather than English; and without fail, for the next dozen years, they returned to Austria each summer to spend their vacations among the Viennese people whom Emanuel knew and loved. When the construction of Symphony Hall in Boston was finally completed in the late spring of 1900, the Fiedler family moved again, this time to a larger flat on Norway Street. It was in close proximity to the new auditorium at Huntington and Massachusetts avenues, and directly opposite Mary Baker Eddy's Mother Church of the Christian Scientists, the construction of which was begun the year Arthur was born. For five years, baby Rosa remained in Austria with her maternal grandmother, and when the entire family returned to Boston for the 1902 Boston Symphony Orchestra fall season, they moved into a large wood-and-stone two-story house at 35 Kenwood Road, in the Fenway section of the city. Within two years, they moved across the street to 36 Kenwood Road, where Arthur spent most of his recollected Boston childhood, from ages eight to thirteen.

Emanuel had two brothers who later followed him to America and also joined the Boston Symphony Orchestra. Bernard — known as Benny — played the violin with the orchestra for forty-five years, until his death in 1942. A bachelor, with a reputation as a ladies' man, Benny lived on Columbus Avenue in Boston and later bought a house on Mason Terrace in the Boston suburb of Brookline. Gustave Fiedler, the youngest brother, married and divorced Johanna's youngest sister, Bertha, prior to joining the Boston Symphony after the First World War. He remained only a short time, choosing to become a teacher and orchestra leader of small ensembles playing at various small hotels and private engagements in and around the Boston area. In 1935, Joseph Zimbler, a cousin from Pilsen, Czechoslovakia, joined the Boston Symphony Orchestra and played cello for twenty-five years, until his death from leukemia in 1960. From 1885, four years after the founding of the BSO, until 1979, the year of Arthur's death, there was always a Fiedler in the orchestra. No other family in musical history can claim a ninety-four-year association with one orchestra. (It could be only a question of time before Arthur's musical education took root and blossomed into a fruitful symphonic career.)

Arthur's early schooling was rather conventional: Kindergarten at Perkins Elementary on Cumberland Street; Prince Elementary for grammar school when the family moved to Norway Street; Martin School after the Fiedlers bought their Kenwood Road house; Boston Latin, perhaps the city's most prestigious high school and the oldest institution of its kind in the United States.

An unconcerned student, he never graduated, being more interested in roller skating, ice skating, football, baseball, and tennis, which he played at every opportunity on the public courts surrounding his house. Although he played the violin, Arthur felt somewhat indifferent toward music, hating to practice with characteristic passion.

The two youngest Fiedler girls delighted their parents with outstanding musical talent. Together with Arthur, they formed a trio: Elsa playing the piano; Rosa, the cello; Arthur, the violin. (Fritzie had no musical interest but occasionally sawed at a fiddle when the mood struck her.) The three youngest Fiedlers played the standard trio literature of Beethoven, Mozart, and Haydn, forever looking at the clock, wishing to end the torture so they could play outdoors with their friends. Elsa and Rosa became distinguished musicians; Fritzie ultimately taught English in Berlin and, on her return to the United States, acted as a German translator-interpreter for Edward A. Filene, the Boston merchandising tycoon. Arthur discovered the LaGrange Street Police Station and began a lifetime interest in fires and other catastrophes. However, his basic commitment to music led him, in later years, to say: "I never left a concert to go to a fire, but I have reluctantly left a fire to go to a concert."

Arthur and Rosa took piano lessons from Carl Lamson, accompanist for Fritz Kreisler and an eminent teacher of his day, at his downtown studio on the corner of LaGrange and Tremont streets. While he was not intrigued by the lessons, Arthur enjoyed being in Lamson's studio because of its location — next to one of the busiest police stations in all of Boston. He would watch the paddy wagons bringing drunks and hoodlums to jail, listen to the profanity bouncing off brick walls, and dream of someday becoming a policeman or fireman. The fantasy was quickly shattered each evening when his father returned home interested in only one thing: "Did you practice today?"

By nature, Emanuel Fiedler was a quiet, retiring man, strict and inflexible on only one subject: music. Johanna was a natural commander, with a majestic air, and, so it seemed to her children, she was virtually unapproachable. Arthur's relationship with his mother was neither warm nor close. Throughout most of her life, she was a sickly person, embittered and distant from her family. Arthur's relationship with his mother consisted primarily of filial respect and cold devotion. From the beginning he was surrounded by women. Whether or not there was great affection — or even any love at all — between Arthur and his sisters is still a matter of conjecture. In later years, whenever they greeted one another — even after long periods of absence — it was with a kind of familiar disinterest, as if affection and warmth had been inadvertently left out of their heritage.

Anyway, it was up to Johanna to make certain that Arthur practiced the two hours each day that his father demanded. More often than not, the neighborhood would hear her clanging a hand bell from the second-floor veranda, then shouting for him to come home and practice. Since the boy knew there would be trouble if he did not and a reward if he obliged — usually a visit to Keith's vaudeville theater or ice skating on the Charles River — Arthur would drop whatever he was doing and come running.

Arthur practiced in the same room with his three sisters, while simultaneously, his father was teaching violin in another part of the house. His mother's logistical ability amazed Arthur. Often he would speak of the times when all the rooms were occupied, compelling him to resort to the bathroom, closing the door for everyone's mutual benefit. Perhaps it was the memory of those days, with five or six instruments being sawed and pounded at, in individual practice, in one apartment, that caused Arthur, when on tour with an orchestra, to refuse to stay at the same hotel or motel as the musicians. He hated the sound of instruments' being practiced while he was trying to rest or concentrate on a score.

Yankee trading between Arthur and his mother was a nonstop event. He was never spanked for being naughty. House arrest and scoldings were more than adequate forms of chastisement. Even though Arthur was a mischievous child, Johanna spoiled him, often accepting with little comment his rebellious attitude toward practice, his desire to be anywhere but home except during mealtimes, and his penchant for shooting off fireworks and pistols with blank cartridges. The Fourth of July was unquestionably Arthur's favorite day of the year. He would promise to practice without argument for a week if his mother permitted him to attend a Fenway fireworks display. Of course, Arthur always managed to carry their agreement one stop beyond reason: Once he came home reeking of smoke and gunpowder after being expressly forbidden to touch a firecracker

— and was grounded for a week or two, receiving another in the endless rounds of scoldings. However, these small sorties were always worth the punishment they provoked.

Near the end of Kenwood Road stood a Boston firehouse. Arthur spent as much of his free time there as possible. He loved playing with the Dalmatian dogs, discussing events of the day with the burly firemen, running up to the second floor so he could slide down the pole over and over again, and skipping alongside the horse-drawn hook-and-ladder companies leaving or returning from a fire. When he was a boy, Johanna refused permission for him to accompany the firemen, but he more than made up for this disappointment throughout his adult life. Many were the times I rode with Arthur in his automobile equipped with a radio tuned to both the police and fire frequencies. He marveled at the life-and-death decisions being made by a soot-covered white-helmeted fire chief, who directed millions of dollars' worth of equipment with an authority equal to Arthur's when he conducted the Pops.

"Incredible," he would say to me, shaking his head slowly. "Fantastic!"

Arthur and the other three Fiedler children were raised much as any other typical American youngsters, with two exceptions: the rigidity of music practice and the insistence that German be spoken at home. Every Saturday morning, Arthur and the girls were dispatched to language school to learn German in the Gothic script. Since it was the children's duty to correspond on a regular basis with their European grandparents, proper German was the only means of communication. There were dividends, however, and Arthur was to take decided advantage of them during the few years that followed. Each summer the Fiedlers visited Vienna (Emanuel never intended to stay permanently in America), and Arthur found himself becoming more involved in the Continental roots of his ancestry. For an entire year while Elsa studied piano at the Vienna Conservatory of Music, she and Arthur lived at the home of their maternal grandparents.

Emanuel returned to his position with the Boston Symphony Orchestra at the end of the summer of 1905, while Arthur remained in Austria and found himself forced into studying entirely in German. Because of his Saturday morning language classes in Boston, it was much easier for the boy to adapt while in Europe than it might be for another foreign child. And when Arthur returned to the United States to enroll in a six-year course at Boston Latin — where he would study a classical English curriculum and play the drums — he found the regimen of study far easier than most of the other students in his class did.

By 1910, the family had moved again, this time to an apartment on Westland Avenue, just around the corner from Symphony Hall. Arthur was fifteen and in his third year at Boston Latin; Fritzie was nearly twenty; Elsa, seventeen; and Rosa, thirteen. Emanuel had spent the better part of the last twenty-five years living in Boston. In his early fifties and able to secure a modest pension for his twenty-five years of devotion to the Boston Symphony Orchestra, Emanuel desperately wished to return to Vienna, where he could teach and enjoy the remainder of his life. Also, there was the psychological requirement of exposing his children to the cultural advantages of European life, education, and deportment. Complete with their dog Nicky, the entire family set sail on a North German Lloyd liner for Bremerhaven, Germany, ready to begin another school year in Vienna.

"I'd had it with more books," Arthur told me. "Latin, Greek, and algebra were terrible. Rather than cut my throat, I rebelled!"

"What did you do?" I asked.

"I told my father I had no interest in going to school. He replied that I had to decide something to do with my life. Maybe I should consider a career in business. Can you imagine me in business, Harry? I don't know anything about business. Not then. Not now."

Nevertheless, Arthur got a job as an apprentice office boy for a sophisticated German women's magazine, comparable to *Harper's Bazaar* or *Vogue*. He ran errands, did janitorial work, took checks to the bank, typed letters with two fingers, filed memorandums, and was miserable. The job paid approximately five dollars a month — considered generous for an apprentice — and he managed to persevere for something more than three months.

"It was stupid." He shuddered. "Damn, how I loathed it!"

"So, what did you do?" I inquired again.

"Not me," he said, with a chuckle. "My father. Old Emanuel took me aside and said since I didn't want to go to school and journalism didn't particularly appeal to me, there seemed to be only one thing left for me to do with my life: I should seriously consider music. It really wasn't a bad thought. With the magazine I'd become increasingly intrigued by the great musical activity in Berlin. So I told father, 'All right. I'll give that a try.' Believe it or not, it was just that casual."

In September of 1911, Arthur auditioned for one of thirteen places in the Royal Academy of Music in Berlin. He was the last applicant accepted. He was sixteen and a half years old, and thirteen was superstitiously regarded as his lucky number from that time on. Surprisingly, he found himself thriving on academy routine and quickly adapted to its rigors. Arthur studied violin, piano theory, harmony, history, chamber music, and conducting. He was at the Academy six days a week, in addition to practicing at home.

"Willy Hess was my violin instructor." Arthur would smile, with fond memory. "He was once the concertmaster of the BSO from 1903 to 1907 —

"I had Arno Kleffel, too, in theory. He was once the conductor of the Cologne Opera House. How that man loved the great German masters! He believed in direct contact and took us to meet as many living composers as possible. Then Ernst von Dohnányi was my teacher in chamber music. You know, Dohnányi became head of the piano department at Florida State University in Tallahassee. We toured there once. Performed his

'Variations on a Nursery Song,' and afterwards he gave us a real Hungarian party at his home."

Maintaining that some people can accomplish more in a couple of hours' practice than others achieve in five or six times that amount of work on their instrument, Arthur would often cite violin virtuoso Jascha Heifetz, whose father believed if two hours of practice made him good, eight would make him four times better. Heifetz would smuggle magazines into his bedroom and, while sawing away for the benefit of his father (who listened behind closed doors in the next room), would scan the pictures, carefully turning the pages, when he had a few bars' rest.

"I always got away with comparatively little practice, too," Arthur once said on the way to rehearsal. "Some of the boys would practice so long each day they developed calluses on their necks. There were also a few girls there, as I remember. God, Hess hated to teach women! 'They would work themselves to a frazzle,' he'd grumble, 'then get married. They'd take their fiddles and hang them on the wall for decorations.' Hess considered it all such a waste of time for women."

By now the entire Fiedler family had moved to Berlin, because life in Vienna was too quiet after twenty-five years in Boston. Arthur's student days in Berlin were spent, for the most part, carousing and generally raising hell. He depended on his innate talent to pull him through. Always in need of money, Arthur took various jobs playing violin and piano in coffee houses throughout Berlin. He was burning the candle at both ends — studying all day and partying all night. Finally, his father clamped down. In a brief argument over curfew, Arthur announced he was leaving home permanently, henceforth to take care of himself. He rented a furnished room, relished his newly discovered sense of freedom, then slowly began to recognize the harsh reality of being eighteen and alone. Suddenly, staying out all night did not have nearly the appeal it once had; earning a living became paramount. Arthur found work conducting a military orchestra. He was nineteen, in his third year at the Royal Academy, and decided that music was to be his life.

Ultimately reconciling with his family and returning home, Arthur decided to remain in Germany if he was to launch any meaningful career as a musician. With virtually hundreds of opera houses in the country, there was always a need for a teacher, a coach, a third or fourth conductor.

While Arthur was vacationing in Bohemia in the southern section of what is now Czechoslovakia, Archduke Ferdinand, heir to the Austrian throne, and his wife, Marina, were assassinated by Gavrillo Princip in Sarajevo, Serbia. The First World War was about to break out, and Arthur was potentially caught in the middle.

As all of Europe was enlisting in one army or another, Arthur returned to Berlin. He arrived home on August 4, 1914, to discover that Britain had declared war on Germany. The most sophisticated and cosmopolitan city in Europe had suddenly become a den of French and Russian spies. Personally recalling very little anti-American emotion in Berlin, Arthur decided to stay, even though other United States citizens were leaving as fast as they could find available transportation. His situation resolved itself on the night of May 7, 1915. Arthur was playing at a private party when the news arrived that a German U-boat had sunk the British liner *Lusitania*. A number of Americans had been killed when the ship went down, and President Wilson was advocating military intervention. Austria, the country in which Arthur maintained citizenship along with the United States, was beginning to draft into military service every man available. With Albert Stoessel, a fellow Academy of Music acquaintance, Arthur boarded a train to Amsterdam. They took a small apartment and went to find employment. The country was flooded with refugees, and jobs were at a premium. After two months of near starvation, their funds dwindling, they sailed for New York aboard the S.S. *Rotterdam*, arriving in America twenty-one days later. On a sizzling day in July, they took a stifling train ride to Boston, the only place in the United States where Arthur felt he had roots.

But now he was totally alone. What had once been friendly neighborhoods and people were only unfamiliar buildings and unknown faces. He found lodgings in a shabby Back Bay boardinghouse, learned that his Uncle Gustave was playing for the summer at the Atlantic House Hotel in Nantasket — a beach resort fifteen miles south of Boston — and took the ferryboat down to the beach. He found his Uncle Gustave but was disappointed to learn there was no available work for a musician in Nantasket; however, his Uncle Benny Fiedler was leading his own little orchestra at a resort hotel on Nantucket Island. Arthur returned to Boston that night, called Uncle Benny, and was told to bring his fiddle immediately. At Woods Hole, Massachusetts, he took his second ferryboat in as many days to Nantucket Island. Uncle Benny could not pay his nephew, but he did offer Arthur a place in his orchestra, playing for room and board. Arthur spent a thoroughly enjoyable summer on Nantucket, entertaining vacationing millionaires.

"They liked my European manner." He laughed, recalling his humble return to the United States. "Took a shine to me and my playing. Night after night these rich guys gave parties. They'd call me at the hotel and tell me, 'Arthur, come over, bring your fiddle, and play for my guests.' There was all the champagne I could drink, ten-dollar tips (an enormous amount in those days), and delightful liaisons with some of the more enchanting vacationing young ladies from Boston.

"By the time summer was over, I was making more than Benny's other musicians."

On his return to Boston with Uncle Benny, finding steady work was critical. The money Arthur had saved would never last through a cold Boston winter, and he did not have Uncle Benny's Boston Symphony Orchestra season to look forward to. He found another furnished room in Boston, heard from a friend of Uncle Benny's about a hotel job in Springfield, Massachusetts, and took a train west. Three weeks later, while performing during an afternoon tea, he received a long distance telephone call from Charles Ellis, the manager of the Boston Symphony Orchestra. An opening might be available in the second-violin section. Was Arthur interested in auditioning? He certainly was, and after playing for Karl Muck, the conductor, joined the Boston Symphony Orchestra. It was September 1915. Arthur, not yet twenty-one, was a violinist, violist, and a pianist. Only thirty-five years old itself, the Boston Symphony Orchestra opened the fall season at Symphony Hall on October 15, 1915. No one had any idea how auspicious a beginning it actually was for a man destined to become one of the most famous musicians of this century.

Arthur was a devilishly handsome man. His fashionable clothes were tailored in the style of the day; he wore spats, gray kid gloves, and a four-pointed white handkerchief in the breast pocket of his suit coat. He carried an amber-colored ivory cigarette holder. He was considered a debonair musician with a sensitive palate for gourmet cuisine, international wines, and twelve-year-old Kentucky bourbon. He was the perennial bachelor, the bon vivant who never dated a girl more than twice in succession and maintained a most discreet social calendar. With his European demeanor, Arthur was utterly irresistible to the Boston ladies. He rented a rather nondescript Back Bay apartment, decorated it smartly but sparsely, and almost instantly began making considerable side money coaching young, impressionable sopranos. Alert dowagers kept their daughters as far away from him as possible. Staid society did not quite understand Arthur's ways.

In the orchestra, Arthur's talents turned him into a traveling handyman, and he was soon playing a game of musical chairs. He shifted from second-violin to the viola section and, from time to time, was called upon to play the piano. Occasionally, he even performed in the percussion section as a bass drum, cymbals, or triangle player.

Pierre Monteux, Muck's successor as music director of the Boston Symphony Orchestra, had to rebuild the orchestra, which had been decimated by an incipient strike among the players. Major Henry Lee Higginson had founded the Boston Symphony Orchestra in 1881, hoping to create America's first permanent symphonic orchestra with his own personal resources. After years of struggle and devotion, the major accomplished his dream, and he viewed the concept of unionism as the antithesis of art. However, certain members of the BSO continued to talk strike. Boston Symphony wages were substantially below those of New York and Philadelphia. On March 3, 1920, the strike became a reality.

Frederick Fradkin was concertmaster. He and Monteux had been having a long-running personal dispute. Fradkin was pro-union; Monteux represented the side of management. The orchestra was playing a concert at Sanders Theater in Cambridge, Massachusetts. Facilities were rather limited, so Monteux and Fradkin were forced to share dressing room accommodations. The conductor suggested that the concertmaster find other quarters. At the end of the concert, Monteux called upon the orchestra to stand for the traditional bow. Fradkin remained seated. The musicians were stunned. Nothing like this had ever happened before. Tension mounted, and two evenings later, at Symphony Hall, the problem came to a head.

"We were all in the tuning room," Arthur said, "and there was a great deal of hubbub and heated discussion. Finally somebody shouted, 'Those who refuse to go onstage tonight move to this side of the room, and the men who will play go to that side.' Nobody knew just what to do. Some of the players were pacing back and forth, and you could almost hear them thinking, 'Shall I strike or not?' Most of them had families, and it was difficult, whatever the reason, to elect to forfeit salary and steady work. As for myself, I was still single, and because I was sympathetic with the cause I chose to sit out the concert. I mean, I guess I just went along with the excitement — as did about half the others. So, Monteux was left with only fifty players, the rest of us having been fired for refusing to play. Of course the program had to be changed in a hurry: Did he have a bassoon? Did he have any clarinets? Did he have an orchestra at all?"

Monteux emerged from the wings to play for a full house with less than half a Boston Symphony Orchestra. Upon reflection, Arthur felt a strike had been totally unfair to the subscribers. Any grievances should have been settled during the between-seasons interval, and the musicians' frustrations not vented on the audience. The following Monday morning, Arthur presented himself to William H. Brennan, the new orchestra manager. He apologized for his actions the previous Saturday evening and stated he still felt he was a member in good standing of the orchestra. Arthur was the only striking member of the BSO accepted back into the fold, thus making him the only Boston Symphony Orchestra musician ever fired and then rehired.

*   *   *

Life for Arthur again became reasonably good. The Roaring Twenties descended upon the country. The First World War was over. Peace was at hand. Arthur was beginning to come into his own. Talented and ambitious, he was bored and disappointed by his lack of rapid progress in the orchestra. He considered — but only for a brief period — leaving Boston for some kind of theatrical job in New York. During the summer of 1921, he made his first and only try at Broadway. Playing rehearsal piano for a new musical, *Chu Chin Chow,* Arthur became so disenchanted that he took the Midnight Special back to Boston, never again to consider a change, but confident there had to be other avenues he could explore musically without jeopardizing his standing in the BSO.

Whether the Cecilia Society sought Arthur out or the other way around is not clearly understood — but Arthur seized the opportunity to conduct. Comprised of both professional and amateur singers from the greater Boston area, the Cecilia Society gave several concerts each year and occasionally collaborated with the Boston Symphony Orchestra.

*   *   *

In 1919, Arthur met the actress Jeanne Eagels, and during the next decade, the Yankee Sarah Bernhardt drifted in and out of Arthur's life. Jeanne Eagels was a beautiful girl — lithe, elegant, blonde, and blue-eyed. She was playing opposite George Arliss in *Alexander Hamilton*, a play destined for Broadway. She and Arthur were immediately attracted to each other. Arthur followed Jeanne's career through the next ten years as she starred in one David Belasco production after another. As Sadie Thompson in Somerset Maugham's *Rain*, she became one of the theater's great success stories, but unlike Arthur, she drank immoderately. They saw each other as often as possible. During a summer holiday in Paris they considered turning the occasion into a great party. However, Arthur possessed neither the disposition of a drunk nor the urge toward self-destruction. On the contrary, by now he was a man who clearly understood where he wanted his career to go and the necessary steps required to get there. Jeanne could not separate her work from play. Her behavior became increasingly mercurial. One moment she was distant and unyielding; the next, warm and loving. She would isolate herself for days at a time, permitting no one to know of her whereabouts; and rumors were rampant that she had become a drug addict. Unable to cope with her melancholia, Arthur began seeing less and less of her, until their relationship ended a year or so before her death in 1929 from a reported overdose of barbiturates and alcohol. She was thirty-four years old, and by this time there were few to mourn her passing.

*   *   *

During Arthur's tenth year in the Boston Symphony Orchestra, Serge Koussevitzky became its conductor. Arthur respected the maestro's extraordinary talent, but found the new conductor lacking the warmth of his friend and advisor, Pierre Monteux. Arthur's ambition to conduct was, by now, much stronger; but he could never muster the courage to consult Koussevitzky with regard to the direction his career should take. He accepted an invitation to become the conductor of the MacDowell Club, an orchestra comprised primarily of semi-amateurs. At about this time Arthur formed the Boston Sinfonietta — a name he coined himself — and hired twenty-two of his Boston Symphony Orchestra colleagues.

For the next several years, the Sinfonietta played in and around Boston, giving Arthur considerable exposure as a conductor. It also permitted the hierarchy of the Symphony to recognize his talent and possibly consider him as the next Pops conductor when the post once again became open. In 1926, Agide Jacchia resigned the podium before the last Pops concert of the season. Arthur was given his big chance. Conducting the Boston Pops for the first time, he closed the program with "Stars and Stripes Forever," the march that — forever — would become associated with the Arthur Fiedler legend. The following morning, Arthur applied for the permanent position of conductor of the Boston Pops. He was turned down in favor of a well-known Italian, Alfredo Casella, who was far more famous as a composer than as a conductor. In the twenties, American musicians were looked upon as no more than apprentices to their European *masters,* and as far as conductors were concerned, no symphonic audience in the country was prepared to accept anyone but a famous European name.

Alfredo Casella's three-year stint as conductor of the Pops was a disaster. He had no feeling for the atmosphere of the Pops. He filled his programs with dull, uninteresting pieces — some old, some new — and none familiar to the audience. In addition, he had a penchant for playing his own material, compositions he had written over the years, none of which had ever been heard in the United States. During the Pops seasons of 1927 and 1928 it became apparent to the Symphony management that, notwithstanding the prestige of their conductor, people were staying away in large numbers. Casella was dismissed. In desperation, they turned to a thirty-four-year-old native Bostonian, the first American ever to conduct the Pops. On February 3, 1930, Arthur Fiedler became the conductor of the Pops. His appointment to the position was carried as a single paragraph on the Associated Press wire:

BOSTON, MASSACHUSETTS, Feb. 3 (AP) — Arthur Fiedler, widely known symphony orchestra musician, will be the conductor of the Pops concerts at Symphony Hall next spring, Symphony Hall officials announced today. He will be the first Bostonian conductor of the Pops.

It will probably come as a surprise to some to discover that Arthur Fiedler was not the *first* Boston Pops conductor. Although his name became synonymous with the Pops during his fifty years as conductor, he was actually the Pops' eighteenth conductor. "The Boston Symphony Promenade Concerts" were begun in 1885, the first conductor was Adolf Neuendorff, in the original home of the BSO, the Boston Music Hall, now the Orpheum Theatre. In 1900, when the orchestra moved to its present home, Symphony Hall, the Promenade Concerts became "The Symphony Hall Pops," and after that merely "The Boston Pops." None of the first seventeen conductors ever approached the success and popularity of Arthur Fiedler.

Arthur did not attempt to change either the format or the pattern of the established Pops program. He merely revitalized it. The three segments, with two intermissions, remained. The first two parts of the program still contained classical or semi-classical music; however, Arthur's first consideration was the audience. They would squirm and whisper no longer. He gave them lively, tuneful music and, whenever possible, works that were familiar. Occasionally, he would include a movement of a symphony in the first section and, from time to time, an entire concerto in the second section. But it was in the final section of the program where Arthur broke new ground. Fiercely anti-snob, he was fond of quoting Rossini: "There is no bad music, only the boring kind!" Consequently, he began playing the current popular music of the day and engaged a young and talented arranger by the name of Richard Hayman to write symphonic arrangements of the material he wished to present. Hayman was responsible for much of Arthur Fiedler's successes through the years, and we are still playing several of Richard's arrangements today. In Symphony Hall's upstairs library there are three large cabinets filled with Richard Hayman arrangements — the compositions number into the thousands. Eventually, Arthur engaged several other arrangers. The late Jack Mason was one, the talented Eric Knight another. Both men contributed richly to the Pops library.

However, the discovery of Leroy Anderson was one of the greatest influences upon the success of Arthur Fiedler and the Boston Pops. Anderson came to Arthur as a fresh, penniless graduate of Harvard with a piece called "Fiddle-Faddle." Arthur was so enchanted by the music that he not only played it, but also recorded the composition, thus beginning Leroy's rise to fortune as a composer of light classical music. Arthur frequently performed many of Anderson's later compositions and arrangements, making Leroy's estate enjoy one of the highest American Society of Composers, Authors, and Publishers (ASCAP) ratings in the country. Arthur never received remuneration from Anderson's publishers, although he occasionally remarked to me that he thought they could have done better by him than sending "a lousy necktie each Christmas."

Now more than ever, Arthur, with his knowledge of German, his smattering of French and Italian, his European mannerisms, and his promiscuous wit, was indeed the irresistible bachelor. He was invited everywhere, sought after by society hostesses and party givers. His speech pattern took on a kind of Boston-Harvard-European accent that was to sustain him the remainder of his life, and it made many of his acerbic comments sound benign.

*   *   *

My first meeting with Arthur occurred in 1931, when he had been conducting the Pops a little more than a year. I was on my way to study at the Royal Academy of Music in Berlin — the same school Arthur had attended some years earlier. After a Pops concert, I was taken backstage to the Green Room — the first floor area in Symphony Hall off the stage used by the conductors for small receptions and intimate conversation. I shook hands with him and told him I was leaving for Germany. He asked me to deliver a five-pound package of coffee to his parents in Berlin. Coffee was very scarce at the time, and I was glad to oblige the simple request. For years afterward, there was a standing joke between us. Upon entering Germany I was charged seven marks duty on the coffee. In American money, this translated into perhaps a dollar seventy-five. Often Arthur made a gesture to pay me by putting his hand into his pocket. Immediately I would refuse, and his hand would always remain there.

Arthur's parents received me graciously and were overjoyed about the coffee. Emanuel, by then in his late seventies, was vigorous and fit. Johanna remained in her bedroom, and other than the introduction and a brief conversation, I never saw her again. The elder Fiedler insisted upon showing me the sights of Berlin. We strolled along the beautiful Kurfürstendamm, with its elegant cafés, restaurants, and shops — Arthur would later speak fondly of this Berlin street and the many nights he had partied until dawn along this thoroughfare — conversing, for the most part, about Arthur, for whom he glowed with pride, the Pops, the Boston Symphony Orchestra, which had been an integral part of his own life for more than twenty-five years, and about music in general.

To all the Fiedlers music was not simply a way of life; it was the very air they breathed. It was their religion, their reason for existence. Nothing else mattered — not even the life-and-death decisions made by an inept German government so riddled by deceit and corruption that inflationary catastrophe would shortly bring Adolf Hitler and Nazism to power. This was of absolutely no concern to them. Emanuel looked much as Arthur would in later years — handsome craggy features and bleached-white mustache; we moseyed along the wide sidewalk of the boulevard, he talking, I listening. I remember that he stopped, tapped his magnificently ornate cane on the side of a wooden lamp post, and said, the hint of a smile at the corner of his lips: "Nice piece of wood. Make for a good violin."

Finally, we sat at an outdoor café in the warm afternoon sunshine. All my life I had dreamed of playing violin for the Boston Symphony Orchestra. The stories old Mr. Fiedler told only made the desire more acute. We drank coffee and ate pastry — very rich and delicious, as I remember. We sat for a while longer, chatting, watching the pedestrian traffic. As we were about to leave, the old man nudged me, pointed his walking stick toward the street and quietly asked, "Do you have such beautiful women in Boston?" Like his famous son, Emanuel Fiedler's eye had never dimmed.

"Dear Little Devil"

F OR SOME MEN, their home is their castle. For Arthur Fiedler, his home was his hotel. Between the Pops, Boston Symphony Orchestra, the Esplanade Concerts, the MacDowell Club, the Cecilia Society, and the social commitments numbering in the hundreds, Arthur was seldom at home, except, perhaps, to change his clothes. As a self-sustaining bachelor, his work habits were of no particular concern to anyone, save his adoring public, who forever demanded more. Prior to meeting Ellen Bottomley, Arthur claimed to have had only one serious romance. Even Jeanne Eagels was a lark. Granted, the relationship extended over a long period of time, but neither of them was serious about anything other than their own careers. However, in the summer of 1927, during one of Arthur's frequent European holidays, he met a girl named Pearl Lebec. It was at the Café de la Paix in Paris, when the world was very young and gay; and the romance would endure for more than six years.

In many ways, Pearl reminded Arthur of Jeanne Eagels. She was blonde, blue-eyed, petite, witty, barely eighteen, and fluent in three languages. Up to that time, she was the most beguiling girl he had ever known. They were practically inseparable during that hot Paris summer of 1927, being seen everywhere. They went to parties with Fitzgerald and Hemingway, ate Alice B. Toklas cookies with Gertrude Stein, enjoyed Comédie Française and the Paris Opera's summer season, took long walks down the wide boulevards and narrow back streets of the Left Bank.

In spite of himself, he promised to meet her again the following summer. It was a scenario Arthur intensely disliked — forever played, he thought, against a backdrop of misty eyes and badly out-of-tune violins. This time, however, instead of the inevitable gloom, Pearl smiled happily, thoroughly delighted to order apéritifs and hold hands.

"When the girls started to get that cow-eyed expression," he once told me, smiling wistfully, "I knew it was trouble."

"What would you do?" I asked, knowing the question was expected of me.

"Look elsewhere," he replied laconically. "And quickly!"

But Pearl was different. She indeed had "the look," but Arthur did not protest. Instead, he was delighted to learn he would not have to wait a year to see her again. In fact, she was going back to America with him, sailing the following day on the *Europa* to New York, where she was to work as an interpreter. He was not quite sure how to accept this news. Totally committed to his independent life in Boston, he tried to explain to Pearl that they would have very little time for each other once they returned to the United States. Undaunted, she said it did not matter. She would be living and working in New York, and they could see each other when the orchestra played in Manhattan. To Arthur's way of thinking, this was a perfect arrangement. Two hundred miles would separate them, and she was content not to disturb either his lifestyle or his career. Indeed, it was the best of all possible worlds.

Before returning to Boston after the *Europa* docked in New York, Arthur introduced Pearl to his sister Elsa, now a professional pianist. Evidently they liked each other from the beginning, and Elsa took Pearl under her wing until the French girl got herself established.

Arthur and Pearl wrote each other from time to time, tele-phoned whenever the mood struck, and he permitted the rela-tionship to remain a constant factor in his life. The following summer, they returned to Paris, but did so separately. Pearl wished to see her mother, and Arthur was not free until after the Pops season ended. Together, they traveled to Berlin. Just as Elsa had in New York, his entire family took an immediate liking to the girl. After a few days, Arthur and Pearl rented an automobile and toured the Continent through mid-September.

"I think it was at this point," he recalled, "that I noticed the subtle changes. Carefree and content became moody and pos-sessive."

"What did you do?" I repeated, again recognizing the ques-tion was required of me, although I admit to being more than casually interested.

"What I always did," he said, with a shrug. "Withdrew."

Arthur returned to Boston; Pearl to her apartment in New York. His schedule became more hectic. The letters and tele-phone calls became fewer and at longer intervals. Then one day she called to tell Arthur the company she worked for was trans-ferring her to Boston. He could not very well tell her to stay away; however, he certainly did not encourage the move north. She arrived six weeks later, settled into a Back Bay apartment, and maintained her discreet relationship with the conductor of the Pops. Scandal-sensitive Beacon Hill began to talk. Idle gos-sip became a proliferation of questions with no answers. Who was the girl occasionally seen in Arthur's company? Was she German? Of course, his family lived in Berlin. No, she was French — just look at the clothes. Who was her family? Did they have money? Surely they must be very wealthy. Arthur was interested only in girls of proper background.

This was the one time in Arthur's life that he became fallible. Arthur wanted to keep his independence, but at the same time, he wanted Pearl available whenever he desired her. However, Pearl also happened to be dating Freddy Church, a former husband of one of the Vanderbilts. When Arthur heard about this he felt wounded. He sent his colleague, Hans Werner, a fellow Boston Symphony member, to plead on his behalf. But to no avail. Pearl told Werner that she was tired of Fiedler's selfishness and that she was going to marry Church.

In later years Arthur never talked about her, never even mentioned her name. When questioned about her he remained noncommittal. "Let's call her 'Amie,'" he would say, "and leave it at that."

The breakup of his romance with Pearl was perhaps the only time in his life when he went through a period of real misery, a time when he might have actually succumbed to marriage if only Pearl would come back. But it was too late — Pearl was forever lost to him.

٭ ٭ ٭

By now, Arthur was the toast of Boston. Definitely the most eligible bachelor in the city, he patterned his life around the uncertainties of the Great Depression and the grueling schedule he maintained. It seemed that every evening there was a different dinner party, and every night a poker game with his cronies. Like many musicians, Arthur was a consummate gambler, an excellent amateur poker player. Always a man who could hold his liquor, Arthur drank judiciously. He loved beer, gin, and most of all, Kentucky bourbon. He drank every day of his adult life, but rarely to excess — except at parties. Before lunch, the big meal of the day, he would pour himself a small tumbler of Tanqueray gin. Occasionally, after I drove him home, he would insist I stay for lunch and pour us drinks in the pantry off the front hall. Knowing I dreaded the taste of gin and was never much of a drinker, he would hand me the glass, lift his in my direction, and say: "Be a man, for God's sake, Dickson! Drink it down. It's good for you."

In the evening before he left for a concert, regardless of whether it was Symphony Hall, the Esplanade, or on the road, he never forgot his silver pocket flask of Old Fitzgerald bourbon. He would carefully lock it away, and from time to time, take a nip before the concert and during intermission. Afterward, in the Green Room, he would enjoy three or four glasses of beer, straight from the tap. The Michelob beer machine was a gift from the musicians, and the dispenser was constantly replenished by the Symphony management. He also kept bottles of Heineken in the refrigerator in case of emergency.

Once the brilliant Puerto Rican pianist Jesús Maria (Chuchú) Sanromá, a frequent performer at Pops, observed: "If I drank like that, I wouldn't be able to play a note. But Arthur always knew when to drink and exactly how much. The only way we could ever tell he might be getting high — say, late at night after a concert — would be when he'd become unusually talkative. One time," he continued, chuckling, "we were all in a jovial mood after the concert and gathered in the Green Room for drinks and sandwiches. Earlier that evening I had gone shopping and left several bags of fresh vegetables on top of the upright piano in the Green Room, planning to take them home after the concert. Arthur noticed the brown paper bags, dug into the sacks and began tossing vegetables all over the Green Room. By now, everyone was on his third drink. Before long we were all wearing vegetables on our heads. Arthur sat at the piano. We all danced around. It was like a living salad bowl in a madhouse, and I don't know what my family ate for dinner the next day. I've often thought poor old Major Higginson would have turned over in his grave if he'd have seen the Green Room on that particular night."

*   *   *

Periodically, Arthur was asked to direct the Vincent Club, an exclusive Boston society group made up mainly of members of the Junior League, who presented charity musical shows. In January 1932, a young girl by the name of Ellen Bottomley was part of the cast of *Spanish Lady*. She was to wave a fan as the orchestra played. During the dress rehearsal Arthur kept glaring at her.

"You," he shouted, pointing his baton in Ellen's direction. "You with the fan. Kindly wave it in time with the music!"

"Me?" she recalled asking, mortified.

"Yes, you," he growled. "In time with the music."

After the rehearsal, they were formally introduced by a mutual friend. Arthur shook her hand, nodded, and inquired if she was the same little Ellen Bottomley he had been introduced to many years ago.

"I was shocked," Ellen told me. "He actually remembered. I was seven years old. Arthur was coaching this very dear lady, Mrs. Olie Fuller, wife of Alvan T. Fuller, governor of Massachusetts, who lived across the street from us. She was a frustrated singer, and then married and became the mother of children, but she never, never gave up that desire to sing. So Arthur, before he went to rehearsals, would go in and accompany her, work with her in the morning, and her daughter was a very dear friend of mine. I had spent the night with Lydia and as we were going downstairs to breakfast we went in to say good morning to her mother. As Mrs. Fuller saw me she said: 'Oh, there's little Ellen Bottomley; good morning, Ellen darling!' So I went forward. In those days you were brought up to make a little curtsey and that sort of thing, and she said, 'Oh, Ellen dear, I don't think you've met Arthur Fiedler.' And so he got up and said 'How do you do' in his gallant way. And that's how we met when I was seven."

However, it was not until many years later that the romance — at least in Ellen's eyes — would truly begin. Arthur had occasion to escort Ellen to a buffet supper after a Boston Symphony Orchestra performance. They sat in a quiet corner, balancing plates on their knees, and became acquainted. During his annual trip to Europe the following summer, Arthur sent numerous picture post cards with cryptic messages. They surprised and pleased her. On his return in September, Ellen's mother refused permission for them to see each other. He was much too old and too wild, her mother insisted. Later, she relented, and if Ellen wished to see him, he was welcome in the Bottomley home. Thus began a nine-year courtship, so clandestine in nature that many people still believed Arthur was emotionally involved with Pearl. Adding fuel to the fire was the perpetual talk of Arthur's affairs with other women, his burning the candle at both ends.

As if that were not enough, there was also the question of religion: Ellen was a Catholic; Arthur, a Jew. Ellen's family refused to acknowledge their love in any light other than a passing fancy. At one point during the late thirties, Ellen became engaged to a West Point graduate, a year her senior, from a very good Catholic Boston family. Still desperately in love with Arthur, she felt like a traitor when the young army officer bought her a diamond ring. Ultimately, the lieutenant was killed during the very early days of the Second World War. It was then that she began to insist to her family that she would marry only Arthur Fiedler.

Arthur and Ellen battled continuously during those years. Each fight would end in a kiss, but it was obvious that they were miserably unhappy. Ellen was determined to marry him. He was forty-five years old, nearly two decades her senior, content with his single life, and inclined to be stubborn.

Two more years passed. Ellen was tired of waiting. She decided to move to New York City to study acting. Arthur was disturbed, as she had hoped.

"This isn't going anywhere," she said when he confronted her.

"Then I'm stuck," he said. That was his proposal. And she remained in Boston.

If the religious differences could be settled, Ellen finally had her family's permission to marry Arthur. The date was set for October 3, 1941. A dozen times it was postponed. The Japanese bombed Pearl Harbor. Father Harry M. O'Connor, Administrator of the Boston Cathedral of the Holy Cross, demanded that

Arthur renounce his Jewish faith. Arthur told him to go to hell. Although he was not a religious man, he did consider himself a Jew, and to deny his Judaism was out of the question.

"What's the difference?" I asked one day after rehearsal. "You love the girl, you sacrifice, right?"

"Wrong!" Arthur stormed. "I may not be a good Jew now, but I may want to take it up one day. Besides, it's strictly my business. The Catholic Church doesn't have a damn thing to do with it!"

"Then why'd you agree to permit the children to be raised Catholic?" I asked.

"I'm forty-eight years old. At my age I don't expect to have any children."

Suddenly Ellen became very ill with a strep throat, and a warm climate was prescribed by her doctor. She left for Pinehurst, North Carolina, where she spent the next few weeks recuperating; but before departing, she arranged to have Louise, Arthur's elderly housekeeper, with whom she had been battling for some years, return to Arthur's apartment and care for him while she was gone.

Father O'Connor conferred with William Cardinal O'Connell, Archbishop of the Boston Diocese and an acquaintance of both Arthur and the Bottomley family, about granting a special dispensation for their marriage. Cardinal O'Connell told them permission for their marriage would have to come from the Vatican; however, since Europe was at war, their case could be taken to the Pope's emissary in Washington, D.C. The formal document of consent was granted. No recantation of Judaism was required. The wedding date was set for January 8, 1942.

But the evening before the wedding it was nearly canceled again. They were returning home from a cocktail party at the Ritz-Carlton Hotel, discussing the pending ceremony in the morning, when Ellen explained that Father O'Connor would read the words in simple English, then they would kneel while the priest blessed them.

"The hell you say!" Arthur shouted. "Kneel? Not me!"

"But all the arrangements have been made," she pleaded.

"Never," he repeated and, without another word, took her home. Shortly before midnight, he called Ellen to ask, "Are we getting married?"

"I don't know," she replied, and hung up.

Calling her back again, he repeated, "Are we getting married?"

"I hope not!" she cried angrily.

"Precisely the way I feel," Arthur countered.

"Well, it's mutual, then," she shouted.

"Whatever happens, dammit, I'm not going to kneel."

Meanwhile, Arthur's family had refused to attend a Fiedler-Bottomley marriage. While they had never been particularly orthodox in their Judaism up to this point, they suddenly rebelled at Arthur's marrying a Catholic.

"Why don't you get married by a rabbi?" Emanuel asked.

"Because she is more Catholic than I am Jewish."

The Fiedler family, all now living in Boston, finally compromised by consenting to attend the reception following the wedding ceremony.

The day of the wedding, Ellen sent her brother George, who would be their best man, to Arthur's apartment. His instructions were simple: He was to stay with Arthur and bring him to the church. Otherwise, she was positive he would never appear. George fortified Arthur's confidence with several shots of straight bourbon. They drove to the cathedral in George's car. Only the immediate members of the Bottomley family were there. Ellen wore a simple red dress and stood beside Arthur. When she knelt to receive the various blessings, he stood rigidly by her side, arms folded. After the lengthy blessings had ended, Father O'Connor finally said: "You may kiss the bride."

"How do you do, Mrs. Fiedler," replied Arthur, and led her out of the rectory into the winter Boston sunshine.

A wedding brunch was held in the home of Ellen's mother. Ellen had invited only a few of her closest friends, but the

Fiedler clan arrived en masse: old Emanuel (who really liked Ellen and told her how happy he was to have her as a new daughter-in-law), Arthur's sisters, and cousins, Josef and Erna Zimbler, their wives and husbands. While all toasted the bride and groom, Arthur and Ellen left by train for a luxurious suite in the Hampshire House in New York.

They arrived in New York late that afternoon, and, fully expecting to be wined and dined, Ellen dressed for a night on the town. Instead, Arthur walked her down Seventh Avenue to where the street crisscrossed Broadway to Lindy's, where they ate cheesecake with a few members of the Boston Symphony Orchestra, in New York to do a chamber music concert at Carnegie Hall. Arthur chatted with them about everything except his new marriage, and Ellen was miffed over the entire affair.

The next evening, Arthur and Ellen hosted a lavish party in their suite for their Manhattan friends. Everyone was happy until Arthur received the bill; Ellen recalls that Arthur's hand was shaking badly as he signed his name to the check. Returning to Boston on Saturday morning because Arthur had a rehearsal with the Cecilia Society on the following Monday, they taxied to his Marshall Street apartment to begin their married life together when they received an urgent message: Uncle Benny was dying. They spent their first evening in Boston at the hospital, and several days later the elderly violinist succumbed to cancer. Benny's funeral was the first time Arthur had ever been inside a Jewish funeral chapel.

One day in 1943, thirteen months after their marriage, Arthur fell ill. He was due in New York for an NBC radio concert that night, and despite her protests he persuaded Ellen to drive him to the airport. She was relieved to hear the broadcast aired on schedule, and assumed that he must be all right. But after the concert a friend called to tell her that Arthur was not feeling well and would spend the night at the friend's home. The next morning, Arthur called Ellen and asked her to pick him up at

Logan Airport. She put him to bed for the next day and night. The following morning, she insisted on calling the doctor, and when Dr. Samuel Levine arrived and ordered an ambulance, Arthur was too sick to protest. He was having his first coronary attack. On the way to the hospital, Arthur told Ellen, "If I survive, I'll stop smoking cigarettes."

For ten days, no one was sure whether Arthur *would* survive. He pulled through and did indeed stop smoking. Soon after that Ellen became pregnant. When the big day came for her to tell Arthur, he just looked at her and said, "But I thought we were happy the way we were."

They did have a lot of fun together. They loved to indulge their mutual passion — chasing fires. Sometimes they would spend an entire night in a fire station awaiting another Cocoanut Grove Night Club disaster, which Arthur had not only attended, but had assisted in helping the victims.

One morning Ellen's mother was stunned to see a front-page newspaper photograph of her daughter, eight-and-a-half-months pregnant, stepping onto a hook-and-ladder fire truck. She was holding her stomach in an effort to get her leg up on a rung, while Arthur beamed down at her from the ladder.

They loved to take walks down all of Boston's finest streets — Boylston, Newbury, and Beacon. He would always dress in his tattered raincoat and brown shoes, hoping no one would recognize him.

After the birth of their first daughter, Johanna, named for his mother, Arthur and Ellen spent more time together. Because the baby was born on the day of Yom Kippur, 1945, Arthur, with his cynicism, and Ellen, with her sense of humor, nicknamed the girl Yommie. Over the years it was changed to Yummie because of the New England way of pronouncing the letter *o*. His acquaintances were astonished at the great change in Arthur. He had suddenly become domesticated. Another daughter, Deborah, and a son, Peter, quickly followed. To accommodate the children and four pianos, Arthur purchased a seventeen-room stately Georgian brick mansion at 133 Hyslop Road, Brookline, a wealthy suburb of Boston. It seemed totally out of proportion to the small Volkswagen parked in the driveway. Inside, with the exception of a few good pieces in the living room, the house appeared to be directly descended from the Salvation Army's "rejected" catalogue pages. One sofa was covered by an old woolly rug; a chair was so worn and threadbare that the springs made it impossible to sit on with any degree of comfort.

"I can't explain it, Harry," Ellen would often tell me. "Perhaps it's because Arthur's a self-made man. He still believes he's working for thirty-five dollars a week in the BSO's second violin section."

Arthur and Ellen had separate quarters, apartments on the left side of the house. They faced each other like domestic bookends. Arthur permitted no one but the maid to enter his living space, and on the outer door was a sign that read MR. FIEDLER. Besides sleeping and caring for his own personal habits, two main practices occurred behind that door: studying his music scores and balancing his checkbook. Once Arthur spent an entire night trying to locate a single penny after his monthly statement had arrived from the bank. By morning, he not only had found it but had determined that the bank had been in error. Before he went to rehearsal that day, he stopped to rectify the mistake. To this day, the bank manager is still in awe over his bank's one-cent computer mistake.

Arthur did not become a father until he was almost fifty-one. Although he was an excellent provider he did not pay much attention to his three children. Each played a musical instrument. Johanna (Yummie) was a violist; Deborah, a cellist; and Peter studied the piano and organ. Ellen monitored their practice sessions, but Arthur seldom heard them play — they were too frightened to perform for him. On one occasion, Peter, then in his teens, managed to appear at a Pops intermission with his own rock group. Arthur knew nothing about it. When he heard them he was dumbfounded. "Where the hell did he learn that?" he exclaimed. Whether or not he was pleased, he never said.

"He was a very strict man, very solid, very set in his ways," Peter said, recalling his childhood. "But beneath the gruffness, under the outside imagery, there was a very tender person, with deep tender feelings, not only for his own family, but for all people, all mankind, and I think he transmitted this every day of his life through his music."

"My father was by no means the classical American daddy," Yummie remembered. "When I was a little girl I had no intimate contact with him. He was away a great deal, of course, on tour. But more importantly, he simply had no interest in small children, who, I guess, aren't particularly interesting. Since he was so much older than most children's fathers, it was something like having a grandfather at home — and a European grandfather at that. Certainly he was very strict. He did not take an active interest in our music lessons. He helped us practice once and it must have been frustrating to him, since none of us was talented. He did not want my sister or me to become musicians; he felt it would be very difficult for a woman to have a career as a musician, which was true enough in those days. All in all, I'd say my father seemed much larger than life to me.

"I attended my first Esplanade concert when I was still a baby," she continued. "I suppose my parents thought it wouldn't make any difference if we made noise outdoors. I went to my first Pops concert when I was six or seven. Watching him conduct didn't thrill me or overwhelm me; perhaps I thought all children had fathers who conducted. My parents had made a very real effort to convince us children that we were just ordinary kids.

"When I entered my teens and became more interesting," she went on, "I developed a closer friendship with my father. Though he didn't push me into the music business, he was very happy when I told him I was going into it. He advised me quite a bit about my career; however, I haven't always taken his advice."

Arthur's relationship with his wife, to whom he was married for more than thirty-seven years, was, according to his outspoken, irrepressible mate, a very stormy one, at best. Ellen loved him dearly. In spite of his protests, she hovered over him and paid no attention to his cold, cynical reactions to her devotion. Unlike her famous but emotionally detached husband, Ellen was, and still is, a bubbling spirit of perpetual optimism and humor. Even her occasional outbursts at Arthur were tinged with humor. After a Pops concert one evening several years ago, Ellen, Arthur, and I were sitting alone in the Green Room. All the guests and hangers-on had left. Arthur began his usual tirade against the orchestra, the management, the audience, and everyone in general. Finally, Ellen turned to me and smiled. "You know, Harry, when I married him I knew he was an s.o.b., but I loved him madly. Now, he's still an s.o.b., and I hate him."

"That's the nicest thing you've ever said about me." He smiled, over the rim of the glass. "Let's go home."

Ellen loved to tell stories in his presence, which Arthur found only moderately amusing, although he groused far more than I believe he actually minded. After all, he was the one who liked to refer to wives as "nothing but a nuisance" whenever Ellen was around. One evening, again in the Green Room, Ellen casually mentioned she had recently had a most interesting conversation with the wife of Jean Martinon, the eminent French conductor.

"We were talking about being married to conductors," she told Arthur and me, "and we decided it was less than glamorous. She told me before the concert they won't, and after the performance they can't." Arthur didn't even smile.

Ellen cajoled Arthur into buying her a four-door black Mercedes. When I asked him why such an expensive car, he said, "So she can show off when she drives to the market every day."

Arthur never threw anything away. Unless a jacket, a suit, or a pair of shoes was ten years old, it was not worth wearing. Some of his earlier suits were tailored by Faber of Boston, long out of business, but he still wore them, and he frequented Brooks Brothers from time to time. No garment was ever discarded unless it was so tattered and torn it was impossible to repair. Shortly before his death, Arthur had lost a considerable amount of weight, and his clothes began to outgrow him. Ellen insisted he purchase a new wardrobe. He, of course, refused. What he owned still had years of good wear remaining. Finally they compromised; they would take all his suits to Brooks Brothers and have them altered to the correct size. In the dressing room, Ellen demanded the suit he was wearing and gave him a new pair of trousers and a shirt. He would wear the new outfit home. Only then did she realize that Arthur had pinned his underwear securely about his waist.

Arthur wore elbow patches with professional distinction throughout his career. During a 1974 interview with Heloise for a Sunday *Herald-Advertiser* article, she asked him how old the coat was that he was wearing.

"It's pretty damn old," Arthur replied. "Look at this . . ." He held up his arms to show Heloise patches on both elbows. "They wear these paddings here in Boston," he continued with a serious expression. "They're not sensitive about them at all, really."

When Arthur had his first coronary attack in 1943, he preferred to call it acute indigestion. For the next thirty-six years he had a number of serious diseases to which he paid no attention and from which he always recovered. With the exception of the 1955 Pops season — most of which I conducted — he never missed a scheduled performance. His work was his life. He possessed an unbelievable inner strength, and his recuperative ability was remarkable. A few years before Arthur's death, Ellen told me:

"I get down on my hands and knees, and ask God Almighty every night, 'Let him drop dead on the podium, please dear God.' That's the only wish I have. For this man's sake, for this dear little devil."

"I'll probably go straight to hell," he once said. "It might be a nice place, really. So many of my friends are already there."

"How do you feel about dying, Arthur?" I asked.

"It's going to happen to all of us sooner or later. There's still too much to do. Sickness, for the most part, is mental. I have never been afraid of death. There may or may not be a hereafter. In my opinion, there isn't one, so why worry?"

"There must be something more than good and bad," Ellen insisted.

"Why?" he demanded. "When they made me an honorary chief of the Otoe Indian Tribe in Oklahoma they said a prayer at the end of the ceremony, and it made sense [Arthur had learned it by heart]: 'May the Great Spirit send His choicest blessing on you. May the Sun Father and the Moon Mother shed their softest beams on you. And may the Four Winds of Heaven blow gently on you and all with whom you share your heart and your wigwam.' They don't care anything more about what's going to happen after they die than I do. I'd never want to be reincarnated a thousand times. Once is more than enough for me. I've enjoyed the trials and tribulations of this lifetime. It's always a battle, but an interesting one. It's like giving up, or quitting. Never! I'll keep on working to the end, because when I die, I'm going with my boots on!"

Arthur had no hobbies. His private life was tailored around his needs. Once he tried gardening, but each spring when it was time to plant, Arthur was in the middle of a busy Pops season. There was no time for anything but conducting. He professed a love of the ground, to work it with his hands; however, I never saw him putter in the garden or, for that matter, exercise in any manner. This was a source of constant amazement to me. He was only five feet seven inches tall and stayed somewhere in the neighborhood of one hundred and fifty pounds. He ate what he wanted and when he felt like it. Because of his heart condition, the doctors instructed him never to eat eggs. Yet, perhaps spitefully, he had two eggs for breakfast every morning. The only diet of which he approved was the one written a number of years ago for the drinking man. Arthur thought it made sense. He once threatened to write his own diet book.

"Have you ever written or composed anything, Arthur?" I asked him one afternoon.

"I limit my writing to checks," he replied, folding the music into his black leather attaché case. "And as few of them as possible!"

"How about autographs?" I asked.

"Hate the drudgery of the damn things." He shuddered on the way downstairs to my car. "Makes me wild. You've got to keep people away from you, Harry. If you let them come to you, they'll devour you. It's so old hat to me. The same thing over and over again every concert: 'Oh, it's wonderful this or wonderful that!' If you allow it, the public will take your last drop of blood, sap your vitality completely.

"It's probably the same with the children," he continued, climbing into the car. "I love them, and that sort of thing, but they like what they like, and I like what I like. We never sit around as a family, and you know, I don't miss that, either. Ellen's tried to keep things on an even keel between me and the children. But I'd get damn agitated when I'd come home and hear them practicing. I guess they were scared to death of hitting a wrong note, or something. We've had plenty of scenes. When I'm away, they don't miss me, and I suppose I don't miss them, either. It's their obligation to admire me. But I was too old when they were born, too set in my ways. They never understood the coolness, the distance, the leave-me-alone attitude. But I can be very warm and charming, at times, so I guess that evens the score."

"You are a combination Santa Claus–grandfather figure, Arthur."

"Disgusting, isn't it? I've reached that age when people tell me how cute I am. Or they want to kiss me. I should say no more often. You know, I still can't get used to the idea of Ellen or other people helping me on with my coat, or when I go downstairs one of the children taking my arm. Oh, sure, I like the niceties and the chivalry, but I like my independence more. I hate it when people make damn fools of themselves."

*　　*　　*

Arthur was a fanatic about order. His entire life was a systematic account of everything he did, where he went, how he arrived, and what occurred when he got there. He kept a permanent record of every transaction made during his adult life. Once he suggested adding the running time of each selection to the Boston Pops program; this was turned down. He insisted that his secretary maintain an accurate record of every concert in which he ever performed or conducted either in Boston or out of town with other orchestras. Given a few minutes' notice, he could tell where and when he conducted; the program for any concert throughout his long career; if there was a soloist, and who it was; and the timing of each piece.

Arthur was proud of the fact that he had conducted an enormous repertory of music. At one time he noted he had conducted 103 marches, 98 overtures, 15 symphonies, 22 rhapsodies, 115 concertos, 51 waltzes, 45 musical comedies, and 1120 miscellaneous pieces.

He would sit in the orchestra library for hours perusing scores for mistakes, scolding the librarians when he found a wrong note, a missing dynamic, or even a frayed page. Musical scores were his bible; he treated them with great reverence. In his later years, Arthur began collecting his own scores, and I used to enjoy conducting from them because of his meticulous markings. Strangely enough, he seemed flattered that I would want to use them. He kept an exact record of everything I took, and spent long, silent minutes checking their contents when I returned them after the performance, frequently accusing me of putting my marks in his scores.

Several months before Arthur died, I conducted a concert for him in Montreal, Canada — a concert that, until the last possible moment, he expected to do himself. When I went to his house to pick up his scores, he was in bed and quite ill, but he insisted on checking each score and carefully writing it down on a gigantic pad of memorandum paper which he kept next to his bed.

"Arthur," I sighed, "don't you trust me?"

"Sure," he grunted, without bothering to look at me. "But it must be written down."

(I suppose he had a reason for not trusting me. He knew I took pleasure in stealing his batons, then telling him about it afterward.

"Don't you ever buy any?" he used to admonish me.

"You never pay for them, anyway."

"That's beside the point."

"They give them to you by the gross, Arthur. What's the big deal?"

"They stamp my name on them, too," he groused, knowing full well we had been through the same discussion many times.

"Arthur found a check under his blotter yesterday," Ellen said to me, changing the subject. "It was three months old and for six thousand dollars.")

"Have to put it in the book," he grumbled.

Fiedler was compelled by nature to do what he did by himself for himself. When it came to the smallest details, he left no stone unturned, and he refused all assistance. Even in his own household he insisted on operating things himself. All bills were paid by check, with Arthur's signature. He even took his own cleaning and shirts to the laundry. Everything was receipted. And we have it on good authority that he once asked an airport manager for a ten-cent statement after he was forced to use a pay toilet! Ellen had no access to his checkbook and absolutely no idea of his financial worth. The household was run on a strict budget, with the money doled out as if the family were welfare recipients. Until a few years before his death, Arthur refused to file a joint income tax return. When his accountant finally persuaded him to include Ellen as part of his return, because he was losing thousands of dollars, Arthur complied reluctantly. He brought home the completed forms, folded them to the signature line, and demanded that Ellen sign them sight unseen. While on tour, all bills were forwarded to him, including the gas, electric, telephone, laundry, and all other household bills. Arthur's checkbook never left his possession.

During the Pops season, and between traveling dates, Arthur's office routine seldom varied. Except on rehearsal mornings, he would spend a good part of the day in his small office making programs and answering his mail. Surrounded by his secretary and Symphony staff, telephone constantly ringing, demands for future programs being made from all directions, people coming in and going out, Arthur would suddenly throw up his hands and go home for lunch.

On one of those days, Arthur received an invitation from the White House to attend a ceremony in which President Ford was to present him with the Medal of Freedom. Somehow the invitation was mislaid, and Arthur almost forfeited the honor. But a few days later he flew to Washington and received the medal.

When I walked into his office the next day, the medal was on his desk. "Ugly, isn't it?" he said.

*　　*　　*

Unlike most professionals, Arthur never had a manager. His secretary would handle all the incoming contracts and block out Fiedler's schedule for when he was not performing in Boston with the Pops. Then Arthur would check the list of offers and plan a tour exactly to his liking.

"I have February twelfth available. Mrs. Weingarth, you may tell them to take it or leave it."

They would always take it. Arthur was a guaranteed sellout.

During his lifetime Arthur conducted over 7000 concerts. Often he was not certain about being paid. He would ask Emily, "Did I ever get paid for that concert?"

"No, not yet."

"Take care of it."

On Arthur's tours with the Boston Pops Touring Orchestra, no BSO players went along. Instead, either an established orchestra or a pickup orchestra, comprised of musicians who had auditioned successfully, went on the road. In 1978, the BSO took on the bookings for all outside Pops concerts by the regular Boston Pops Orchestra or the Pops Esplanade Orchestra, the latter made up of first-class musicians who now perform regularly when the Pops orchestra is not available.

Arthur was known for a notorious, lifelong habit: He would enter a restaurant, join his colleagues, have hors d'oeuvres, bread and butter, and leave without paying.

* * *

Was there a point to Arthur's frugality? Was it a portion of his basic insecurity? Was it a psychological crutch he needed to remind him of his early poverty? Arthur and Ben Franklin would have gotten along marvelously well. A penny saved was a penny earned. However, Arthur carried it to an extreme. In a rare moment of generosity, he once invited the Boston Symphony Orchestra's first harpist, Bernard Zighera, and his fiancée, Carol, to a drink at the Ritz-Carlton. It was a bitter cold, wintry day. They arrived in the vicinity of the hotel, and Arthur insisted they all leave their coats in the car to avoid paying for checking. They did so, and almost froze to death as they walked to the bar.

Then there was the poker game in which Arthur lost five dollars. Irving Frankel, a musician with the BSO, related it to me, as follows:

"Several of us were playing poker in the tuning room — idling away some time like we always do between sessions. Arthur came back, asked to sit in, and quickly lost five bucks. Big deal, right?

Well, it damn sure was for Arthur. I kept asking for the money. Each time, he refused to pay, offering one excuse or another. One time he told me he was going to Europe and had barely enough to make the passage. Finally, out of desperation, I guess, I struck a bargain with him. Twenty-five cents a week. It took me twenty weeks to get my five dollars, but it was worth every payment just to see him dig deep into his pocket, grumble, and mutter beneath his breath as he handed me the quarter."

Libby Owen Glass Company once presented Arthur with a glass top for the concert grand. Arthur donated the cover to the BSO, expecting to write it off on his income tax.

He was not even very generous at Christmas time. When I would give the stage-hands presents, Arthur would say, "Trying to get in good with them, Harry?"

Arthur did buy presents for his family. On December 24, he and David Mugar would shop at the Chestnut Hill Mall, where stores like Filene's and Bloomingdale's have branches. He loathed having throngs of people ask him for autographs. It would take him ten minutes to get from his car to the front of the store.

Many times on cold days, Arthur would look at me seriously and ask, "How much does it cost to heat your house? It costs me a fortune."

Whenever Arthur did not go home for lunch, he and Bill Shisler, one of our BSO librarians, would go to the deli across the street from Symphony Hall for corned beef sandwiches and tea. (Bill was, for many years, Arthur's link to the Symphony and Pops library. It was Bill who was in charge of transporting music to the various orchestras Arthur conducted. Of our three librarians, Bill was the closest to Arthur, having even traveled with him and chauffeured him on many of the Fiedler conducting tours. Yet he never addressed him other than "Mr. Fiedler.") As they walked back down Massachusetts Avenue to Symphony Hall, often they would stop at Hutchinson's Market for an apple. Apples cost five cents in those days, and the two men would flip a coin to see who would pay for them. Bill usually ended up buying.

It seems paradoxical, but Arthur never displayed any great, consuming desire to invest his money. He simply could not bring himself to spend it once he cashed the check and got it into the bank. He knew the value of a dollar, forever reminding those around him that he had earned every penny he had the hard way. Once, a little out of desperation, I said, "You know, Arthur, there's an old cliché: 'You can't take it with you.' " (He was said to be earning over a half-million dollars per year.)

"Yeah, yeah, I know. But it's sure damn good to have while you're alive."

*   *   *

Toward the end of each Pops season, Arthur would say to me, "Should I give that damn party again?"

"Why not, Arthur?" I would ask.

"They don't like me. Why should I give them a party?"

Diplomatically, I would try to convince him that he was not as hated as he thought. After all, he was a conductor!

He always made the arrangements himself. He would call the New England Provision Company and have basically the same conversation, year in and year out:

"Hello, Sam? Fiedler, here. It's time for that goddam party again."

Arthur would then consult various slips of paper he had saved from previous years.

"Last year," he would say back into the phone, "we had forty pounds of hot dogs and ran out. These musicians eat like pigs. Let's make it forty-five pounds. I'll be down soon to pick them up."

He would then call the Symphony Deli, located across the street from Symphony Hall, and proceed with his annual conversation, still rereading the crumpled piece of paper in his hand. The deli provided condiments, rolls, sauerkraut, and potato salad.

Once, after he had made these calls, I said, "Arthur, you should be ashamed of yourself."

"Why?" he said, frowning.

"A man in your position going to pick up hot dogs and a free salami!"

"How would you do it?" Arthur inquired.

"Well," I began. "You just call a caterer, tell him how many people are coming, what you want, and he will supply you with everything you need."

"Maybe you can afford it," he said. "You married a rich woman!"

*　　*　　*

He practiced a deep-seated, unabiding avoidance of taxis. As far as anyone knows, he never took one — that is, one for which *he* had to pay. In his later years, Arthur gave up driving. Consequently, he was taken to and from rehearsals and concerts by the Symphony Hall chauffeur, an easy-going, affable man named Paul Kehayias. When Paul was unavailable for the evening performances, our Pops first clarinetist, Patsy Cardillo, had the honor. On days when Arthur did not have to conduct in the evening and spent the bulk of his day in the office, Carol Green, his secretary at the time, was enlisted for the job. One day, while being taken through the Callahan Tunnel to Logan Airport on his way to an out-of-town engagement, Arthur was dozing. He awoke moments before they approached the toll booth, reached into his pocket, found a quarter, and, handing it to Carol, said, "Here, take it. I don't want you to be out of pocket."

"Thank you," she replied, knowing full well that he conveniently forgot that after she left him at the airport she would have to pay another twenty-five cents on the return trip to Symphony Hall.

*　　*　　*

Unlike some artistic people, Arthur was anything but an eccentric. He was never late for anything in his entire life, except, as he was fond of saying, his own funeral. He never pressed a suit, believing if he bought good clothes they required nothing but constant wear.

He loved to tell tales of Uncle Benny, the bachelor-violinist who spent forty-five years with the Boston Symphony. Benny was a clock fancier. Every Sunday, he wound his thirty-five or more clocks, taking the entire morning to accomplish the task. Arthur made certain never to see Uncle Benny on the hour, any hour. The clocks would begin to chime and it was virtual pandemonium.

He would never have anything to do with his cousin, Joseph Zimbler, after Joe organized the Zimbler Sinfonietta, a string ensemble in which I played for a number of years. Arthur had originally coined the word *sinfonietta,* and the fact that Zimbler used it without Arthur's permission and continued to use it after Arthur asked him to find another name was, to Arthur, grand theft. No family ever fought with more relish and zeal than the Fiedlers. Uncle Benny, who boasted that he "lived like a king," was very proud of his nephew, but could never tolerate Arthur's miserly attitudes. Benny lived on Mason Terrace in Brookline, in a lovely home which he always referred to as the house on Mason *Toches,* and could never understand how Arthur spent so much money for a brick mansion, then permitted it to decay. It was like buying a Rolls Royce and never washing it. If anyone asked Benny how much he was leaving Arthur when he died, he would flip his finger into the air and exclaim: "One dollar!" After Benny died without leaving a will, the Fiedler family renewed their feud as they fought over Benny's estate. The only things Arthur was not interested in were the clocks.

(III)

The Pops and Symphony, Light and Serious Competition

Tʜᴇ Bᴏsᴛᴏɴ Sʏᴍᴘʜᴏɴʏ Oʀᴄʜᴇsᴛʀᴀ, like only five or six other major orchestras in the United States, employs its musicians on a year-round basis. This is a rather recent phenomenon. In the early days of the BSO, the musicians' employment was seasonal, and their livelihood was precarious, at best. Even today, the majority of the symphony orchestras in the United States do not have a year-round schedule, and their musicians must supplement their incomes by teaching, playing, or even working in different fields. Obviously, an orchestra cannot possibly find adequate funding to pay a player for a full year when he is actually working only a third of the year.

When the Promenade concerts were added to the Boston Symphony schedule in 1885, it meant ten additional weeks of employment for the players, added to the thirty-week year. This forty-week-employment year lasted until the early forties, when Tanglewood became a fixed reality, and the season was extended to a full year. The present BSO schedule has three subdivisions: Symphony, Pops, and Tanglewood. We also employ the Pops Esplanade Orchestra, made up entirely of first-rate musicians who play at Symphony Hall when the regular Pops is not playing, and who now play all of the Esplanade Concerts.

There is no dearth of musical activity in and around Boston, and Arthur Fiedler used to say, "There's too much of it. You can't get away from it. In elevators, in restaurants, in bars, or on the street — too damn much music."

"There's really no boundary line between different kinds of music," Arthur once said. "One overlaps the other. There is relation in lighter music — and lighter art and lighter literature. And some of the highbrows have now discovered there can be wonderful light music. By the same token, people who have never been to a symphony come to our Pops Concerts and discover that they like the more serious music, too. Many have become regular patrons of the Boston Symphony. A Strauss waltz is as good a thing of its kind as a Beethoven symphony. It's nice to eat a chunk of beef and have a slice of dessert, as well."

The Boston Pops is an integral part of the Boston Symphony Orchestra; yet there has always existed a sense of separation between the two. The players of the Pops, with the exception of a few extra musicians, are all members of the Boston Symphony, under contract to play both the Symphony and Pops seasons. About fifteen first-chair players of the BSO have, by tradition, never played the Pops Concerts. During the regular Pops season, between May and July, these musicians go on tour under the name of the Boston Symphony Chamber Players, then reunite with their colleagues for the Boston Symphony Orchestra summer festival at Tanglewood.

Even in the minds of the trustees and the management there has always been the feeling that the Pops is of secondary importance to the staid Boston Symphony Orchestra. This, in spite of the fact that the Pops shows no financial deficit, in contrast to the inevitable deficit incurred by all symphony orchestras. In fact, the Pops, through its recordings and its radio and television broadcasts, shows a profit and helps reduce the deficit of its parent organization. Moreover, the Pops has been a means of introducing thousands of people to serious music, and to the BSO itself. Yet, the condescension has always existed, and Arthur felt it keenly. It was as though the Pops were the vulgar relative who was tolerated because it paid the bills.

For Arthur's fiftieth and the Pops' ninety-fourth season, Symphony Hall released an extensive program to accompany the concerts. Here is a portion of their version of the beginnings of the Pops:

Since Arthur Fiedler is so closely identified with this enormously successful musical ensemble, many people are surprised to learn that there was a Pops in existence long before he became its maestro.

When Henry Lee Higginson founded the Boston Symphony Orchestra in 1881, he stated a culturally democratic goal. He wrote of his wish to present in the city "as many serious concerts of classical music as were wanted, and also to give at other times, and more especially in the summer, concerts of a lighter kind of music."

Higginson's idea of lighter musical offerings wasn't at all revolutionary. When he made his proposal in 1885, operettas were all the rage and lilting concerts in genteel garden and courtyard settings were in high vogue. It was the heyday of Lehar, Suppe, Sousa, Johann Strauss, and similar contemporaries — the veritable grandfathers of today's "easy listening" musical programming.

Yet the idea was innovative, for Higginson was linking it with the establishment of a major musical organization.

The relaxed party atmosphere that characterizes today's Pops concerts has been employed right from the 1885 beginning. Rows of seats in Boston's Music Hall were hauled aside to make room for tables and chairs. The serving of chilled refreshments combined with a wafting, effortlessly uplifting style of music was welcomed by Bostonians as an ideal summer evening's entertainment.

In 1900 the Orchestra moved to Mechanics Hall for a short period, and then to the magnificent, brand-new Symphony Hall.

That and subsequent Pops history prior to 1930 could be termed B.F. — Before Fiedler. After 45 years, 17 conductors, and several million concertgoers, Arthur Fiedler took command of what by then had become a solidly established city attraction...

From 1955 to 1978, Arthur Fiedler conducted one Boston Pops Concert at Tanglewood each year. This concert usually broke Tanglewood attendance records. Although the Pops was originally intended as an adjunct to the Boston Symphony Orchestra, a means of providing light concerts in contrast to the serious programs of the regular season, and at the same time, giving extra pay to the then-underpaid musicians, during Arthur's half-century tenure the Pops began to compete with the Boston Symphony itself, a situation which by no means appealed to the egomania of Serge Koussevitzky. And Koussevitzky did not hide his feelings. He came to one Pops concert and was horrified to see people casually sitting at tables, drinking beer, and listening to the music with less than the usual reverence accorded *his* orchestra. Invariably, when he returned to the first rehearsal of the Boston Symphony Orchestra at the opening of Tanglewood, he would stop after only a few minutes, and exclaim, "Vot happen to mine orkester? I know. Too much Popst!" He did not like Arthur and, with one exception, never invited him to conduct the Boston Symphony at a regular winter concert series or at Tanglewood. The one exception was an invitation later rescinded. (It was not until Koussevitzky resigned from the orchestra after twenty-five years as music director that Charles Munch, the new BSO conductor, invited Arthur to conduct at a regularly scheduled concert series.) Koussevitzky would also find it difficult to tolerate the ongoing series of popular rock and jazz groups attracting thousands of young people that enlivens Tanglewood.

Arthur's relationship with the trustees and management was always somewhat strained. Although he was among the world's best-known conductors, it never occurred to him to exert his authority. He refused the title of Musical Director, preferring only to be called Conductor. He once told me he had never asked for a raise, and never would.

Although he conducted the Pops for fifty years — and to the general public he *was* the Pops — strangely enough, he never felt secure in his job. For his first twenty-five years he conducted all the concerts, six nights a week for ten weeks each season, without a guest to relieve him. Then, in later years, when the Symphony management realized he could not go on forever, they began to engage occasional guest conductors without his consent. Arthur resented this, but he was too proud to voice any complaints. Actually, he was worried about being fired himself!

*   *   *

In 1955, after a quarter of a century of conducting the Pops without missing a single concert, Arthur Fiedler proved to be mortal after all. Just prior to the opening of that Pops season his doctor told him he required immediate surgery. A lower intestinal tumor had been discovered. He tried to fight the doctor's decision — at least to postpone the operation until the end of the current Pops season — but was finally frightened into giving his consent.

Arthur called me into his office to tell me of his impending operation and his suggestion to the management that I take over until he returned. As far as I know I was the only conductor he ever recommended.

Neither he nor I imagined he would be gone most of the season. The morning of the operation I received a telephone call from the hospital. The tumor was malignant, but there was hope that it had not spread and that it would not recur. Arthur was never told that he had cancer. He assumed the tumor was benign and years later said to me, "I was pretty damn lucky that tumor wasn't cancer." After leaving the hospital he recuperated at home, and for the rest of his life, never had a recurrence of the disease. By the time he returned to the podium for the final week of the season I had learned to admire him for having done so long what I found to be physically and emotionally exhausting to do for just one season. The fact that Arthur managed to do it year after year is still amazing to me.

When I took over the Pops at the beginning of Arthur's illness, the Baldwin Company, the official purveyor to the Boston Symphony and the Pops, delivered a concert grand to my house, and when Arthur returned to the podium they took it back. I remember my wife's exclamation to the movers, "Indian givers!"

At the close of that Pops season I was officially appointed assistant conductor, the first time in over twenty-five years that Arthur had accepted any help. After my appointment I continued to play when Arthur conducted, and he gave me some advice: "Don't talk to the management about money."

"Why are you so suspicious of everyone?" I demanded.

"I have my reasons," he countered.

"Surely you're not suspicious of me?" I asked, genuinely startled.

"Well," he grumbled, "I'm not so sure!"

After I had worked with Arthur for a number of years, our manager, Tod Perry, suggested to Arthur that my title be changed from Assistant to Associate Conductor. However, Arthur flatly disagreed. It was not until after his death, when John Williams was appointed conductor of the Pops, that the trustees of the Boston Symphony Orchestra simultaneously appointed me associate conductor.

I did not really mind being less than an associate conductor during those years. Life was busy. But I did mind Arthur's monopolizing the rehearsal time. He would tell me at the beginning of each rehearsal that the orchestra did not need to go through my pieces because they already knew them. He would then proceed to rehearse a Strauss waltz that we had played a hundred times. Inevitably, I would have at most ten minutes out of a two-and-a-half-hour rehearsal to prepare my own programs.

According to Ellen, Arthur at one time almost came to my defense. We were about to do a Pops Concert at Royal Albert Hall in London when he fell sick. Although I was there, the BSO management flew in Erich Kunzel to conduct. Arthur was furious at the pointed insult to me, his assistant conductor; but his natural disinclination to become involved prevented him from doing anything about it. Later, Ellen took it upon herself to go to the management and scold them; afterward she berated Arthur for his silence.

He really did have a certain aloofness in his relationship with

Symphony management. One of his secretaries once requested a five-dollar raise and asked Arthur to add a few words of support in her letter to the manager. He threw the letter on the floor and told her that although he valued her work highly, he was not going to involve himself in a matter he considered none of his business. She resigned and immediately found a more lucrative position.

In 1949, Serge Koussevitzky had threatened the Boston Symphony Orchestra with resignation and they accepted it. Arthur never forgot that. A number of years later, during a very hot summer, Patsy Cardillo said, "Arthur, you've got to do something about air conditioning. Why don't you threaten to resign unless they put it in?"

"Not me," he said. "You know what they did to Koussevitzky!"

But Arthur found ways to deal with the Symphony by using the press. In 1962, he gave Elliot Norton a story about his cross-country jaunt with the Boston Pops Touring Orchestra. Within the article Norton wrote for the Boston *Record* was a brief paragraph about Symphony Hall's not being air-conditioned. The article appeared, taking Arthur's grievance to the public:

Everything is fine with Fiedler [the paragraph began], or almost everything. The management of Symphony Hall still hasn't agreed to install air conditioning, and that irks him. He resents the fact that Popsgoers, on hot nights, have to make fans of their programs to keep cool, and that his musicians appear coatless because of the heat. "The men should wear coats," he believes. "Without coats they look like a lot of barbers!" But Symphony Hall has never had air conditioning, and the management seems to distrust these new-fangled notions such as making the summer season comfortably acceptable. If the Hall were air-conditioned, it might even be possible to have a second Pops series in July and August, to accommodate thousands of Bostonians and an enormous number of tourists. That people would come to such a series of light pleasant concerts in a comfortable hall stands to reason. The notion that "everyone is away" in the summer is just so much poppycock: Who are all these people in the streets?

Arthur was not actually campaigning for an extended Pops series, though he realized such a series might well attract a large audience. On the contrary, the May through June Pops season was substantial enough. Then, too, in July and August, the Boston Symphony Orchestra was in Tanglewood, which would make it necessary to recruit substitute players. In a relatively short period of time, however, Arthur made his point, and Symphony Hall saw the wisdom of installing this "newfangled notion."

*   *   *

Despite the tremendous popularity of the Boston Pops under Arthur Fiedler, especially during his last ten years, the feeling has persisted among many musicians in the orchestra that the Pops Concerts are somehow demeaning to the musicians and the institution of the Boston Symphony Orchestra. The fact that the same classically trained musicians, who, during the regular season, have been performing Brahms and Beethoven and Stravinsky and Mahler and rehearsing an entire week to prepare each program, are now asked to play "Boogie-Woogie Bugle Boy" or "The Stars and Stripes Forever" every night of the week, causes many players some artistic frustration. Their sensitive feelings are, however, kept in abeyance during the Pops season for a pragmatic reason, that of earning a living.

The Pops has, over the years, also been a psychological reverse status symbol for regular Symphony subscribers who would not be caught dead at a Pops Concert.

One very positive thing that came about through our *Evening at Pops* television series was our close association with a new breed of performers, those who had made it in the popular field. With our classical training, many of us had previously looked upon these "Stars," no matter how successful they were, or how popular, as beneath us. These were "entertainers," not musicians, not artists. They made lots of money; so what? Their appeal was to the masses, the uncultured, the uneducated. And how wrong we finally realized we were! Most of those who appeared with us on our TV shows were true artists in their own right, highly gifted men and women, serious and just as dedicated to their craft as we were to ours. And there was established a mutual respect between us, which I hope will continue in our future collaboration. American popular music has made, and will continue to make, a significant cultural contribution not only to our own country but to the rest of the world.

Outdoor Music
for the People

In 1927, Arthur had begun working virtually alone to bring a great dream to reality: open-air summer symphony concerts, free to the public. The finest literature was accessible through the public libraries, Arthur reasoned. Throughout the world, the masterworks of art were available for a few pennies in museums, which spent money to advertise their exhibits. But when it came to classical music — any music — the public was obliged to purchase tickets. Therefore, Arthur decided, why not bring a series of free summer concerts to Boston? The only question remaining was how to go about creating such a series. In short, who would provide the money?

Arthur broached the subject to acquaintances and to the management of the Symphony. If the response was not out-and-out skepticism, it certainly was scoffed at as being impossible. Free concerts were provided by park bands. Great music was funded by subscription, donation, and the box office where people bought tickets. Besides, no one could imagine substantial numbers of classical music lovers. The Boston Symphony Orchestra was no different from any other symphony orchestra — it lost money every year. Without the wealthy, symphonies would starve. People sitting quietly in a public park just listening? Everyone told Arthur the idea was ridiculous. Return to the viola section and forget it. He smiled and quietly undertook a one-man campaign to prove that there were millions of people who were vitally interested in good music.

Arthur had already chosen the site for his summer series: the wide, flat grassy esplanade near the Union Boat Club on the Charles River Basin where he and his sister Fritzie had gone ice skating when they were children. He compiled a prodigious list of things required to bring the Esplanade Concerts to the people of Boston. First, the moral support — the interest by the Boston Symphony Orchestra Board of Trustees to help him get his foot in the door; second, the necessary funding to lease the site from the city — if the Parks Commission could not be enticed into donating the land for the public betterment; third, some sort of acoustical band shell; fourth, the cooperation of the city's police and fire departments; fifth, money to compensate the musicians; sixth, staging and equipment, such as music stands and the conductor's platform; seventh, the necessary lighting not only so the players could read their music and follow Arthur's baton, but also so the audience could see the orchestra; eighth, seating — perhaps long rows of benches to accommodate several thousand people; ninth, cooperation from the City Fathers; tenth, the planning for solicitation of substantial blocks of money; and finally, one man to lend credibility to what Arthur had in mind.

Alvan T. Fuller, the ex-governor of Massachusetts and an old acquaintance of Arthur's, was approached. Fuller owned the largest Cadillac agency in New England and promised Arthur he would match dollar-for-dollar any money the young conductor could raise. He would also telephone a few friends around town to see what they might do. Arthur now had the man to lend credibility to the proposed venture. Next, he instituted the Esplanade Concert Fund and began knocking on doors, soliciting money by mail and cornering possible contributors at the numerous parties he attended. By the spring of 1929, Arthur had enlisted the support of fifteen important Boston businessmen and had accumulated approximately fourteen thousand dollars — although no one except Fuller showed any real faith in his Esplanade idea. The money was donated, but the donors wished to remain anonymous. However, the legal firm of Lee, Higginson, and Hallowell was in charge of administering the money, and since a Higginson was the founder of the Boston Symphony Orchestra, several important people decided to lend their names to Arthur's dream. Ernest B. Dane, an important member of the BSO board who later became its president, came to the forefront, and none too soon.

At about the same time, Arthur learned that the proposed concert site was not city property but belonged to the Commonwealth of Massachusetts, and state officialdom was not about to donate or lease any property to him. Dane, Fuller, and Arthur went to visit the head of the Metropolitan District Commission, the department that controlled the Esplanade and dictated the policy pursuant to the riverland property. A bargain was reached. Arthur had one year to prove himself. If the concerts were rowdy or had small attendance, the great experiment would come to a halt. Arthur needed no more encouragement. Immediately passing the news along to N. Penrose Hallowell, the man personally administering the Esplanade Concerts Fund, Arthur had a crude wooden acoustical band shell constructed. The cost was something more than two thousand dollars, and Arthur told an acquaintance it was probably the most beautiful sight on earth.

On June 22, 1929, more than two years after Arthur created the plan for the Esplanade Concerts and about seven months before his appointment as conductor of the Pops, the Boston *Advertiser,* under the headline FREE SYMPHONY CONCERTS / Mr. Fiedler to Present Good Music, published a story by Alex Warburton, which reported, in part:

The project of the Esplanade concerts is entirely the result of Arthur Fiedler's efforts during the past two years. So far as it is known these will be the first concerts of the kind in Boston musical history, perhaps in any other location in the world. It is certainly the first time that a large group of Boston Symphony players have performed outdoors. Although only about half of the Symphony Orchestra will be engaged, forty-six players, the group will be large enough to give adequate presentation of popular classics. This has been proven previously by Mr. Fiedler and his Boston Sinfonietta, a miniature orchestra chosen from the Boston Symphony, giving several concerts in Boston and a great many New England cities in the past few years.

Arthur planned five weeks of concerts to be presented six nights a week at 8:00 P.M., beginning July 4, 1929. The Metropolitan District Commission was still skeptical, and their captain of police especially so. The concerts would be nothing more than an open invitation to create a battleground on the Charles River for hooligans from the North and South ends of Boston. There were not enough policemen to protect the city.

With these fears in mind, Arthur had the following note printed on the program of the first concert:

As the success and continuance of these concerts rests with the public, it is hoped that appreciation will be manifested by refraining from making unnecessary noises and the scattering of these programs on the grounds.

An armada of police was on duty that first night, waiting to quell the impending riot. A crowd estimated at five thousand was scattered on the grounds: They stretched out on the grass; some rented chairs for ten cents apiece; others brought blankets. But the human explosion the police anticipated never occurred. The audience was well-behaved. They sat with quiet attentiveness, listening and appreciating the music, which some had never heard. Even the children appreciated the program, and all the doubts attached to Arthur's dream vanished. In fact, the only disruptive note the entire first night was the weather. It was warm, but breezy. The music on the players' stands flew all over the band shell as if the paper had sprouted wings. Stands toppled like wrought-iron trees through much of Wagner's Overture to *Tannhauser,* and during the final selection, Victor Herbert's "American Fantasy," they rolled into the river. Listeners volunteered their assistance. They scrambled about the Esplanade retrieving the musicians' music. Several stood or crouched by the stands, holding the scores in place, and many musicians simply played from memory. Arthur conducted without interruption through it all, making the concert a memorable occasion for everyone concerned and a landmark in the annals of classical music.

Later, Arthur devised a glass plate attached to a lever to place over his score to protect it against the wind, and for the musicians, he invented an elongated wood-and-metal clip to hold down the music while, at the same time, making it relatively easy to turn the page. Climatic conditions, however, were not Arthur's only problem that first night. Immediately after he and the orchestra, resplendent in black coats and white trousers, took their bows, Arthur tackled the real problem — the wooden band shell simply had not done the acoustical job originally anticipated. The string section, the heart of a symphony orchestra, was barely heard beyond the first couple of rows of the audience. The piccolos, on the other hand, were audible above all the other instruments. The drums sounded dead — muted and flat. The horns could not be heard at all except after they had bounced off a brick wall down Embankment Road, rattling Admiral Richard E. Byrd's windows. It was reliably reported that the Admiral believed he was back "in a South Pole wind tunnel" and did not find it the least bit attractive. To rectify this situation, Arthur consulted a structural engineer, who suggested changing the configuration of the band shell. Although this helped significantly, it was not enough to satisfy Arthur. The Esplanade audience still could not hear beyond a few hundred feet from the ochestra.

Finally, Arthur took his problem across the Charles River to the Massachusetts Institute of Technology, in Cambridge. Dr.

William R. Brass (yes, that was really his name!), professor of acoustics, studied the dimensions and angles of the acoustical shell in relation to the logistics of the surrounding area, then directly applied his findings to the Esplanade site. Various instruments were moved about the stage in highly irregular concert positions, thus taking advantage of the natural amplification qualities of the acoustical shell and minimizing the echoing reverberations. The orchestra members took their new positions in utter confusion. Everything was backwards: Instruments normally on the right now appeared on the left, back became front, and everything was topsy-turvy. Who ever heard of brass being situated directly in front of the conductor? But it worked, and the quality of music improved remarkably. To the occasional guest conductor, Arthur would explain the radical orchestra seating and ask him not to be disturbed by it.

By the end of the first season, the Esplanade crowds had grown to approximately ten thousand per night. Generally, the critics were most complimentary. They were, however, somewhat dismayed by the fact that Arthur seemed to be conducting an echo, an extra orchestral sound never heard in Symphony Hall. Yet as if by magic, they unanimously agreed, Arthur was able to gauge precisely the degree of volume and intensity required to reverberate the music off surrounding tall brick apartment buildings and turn a decided disadvantage into tonal emphasis. One reviewer wrote: "Fiedler, through force and timing, caused the echo to perform as an exclamation point by holding the orchestra until the echo returned, before beginning the next part."

Still not satisfied with the shell, Arthur tried another structure for the second season, but it worked no better than the first. The third attempt was a trifle better than the second, but still left a great deal to be desired. Conversation from the audience could be clearly heard on stage. It was not until 1940, when the Hatch Memorial Shell was constructed, that the acoustical problem of the Esplanade was finally solved. During the eleven-year interim between the first Esplanade concert and the beginning of the 1940 summer series, a host of weird things occurred: Rain nearly ruined the instruments. We were invaded by ants, gnats, flies, and mosquitos. On the night of July 25, 1930, a blue horsefly bit Arthur's neck, almost causing him to stop conducting. A bee popped out of Joe Wilfinger's violin. The orchestra suffered a mass of ugly red welts, and one trombonist was overheard by a newspaper reporter to comment: "This is one hell of a way to earn a living!"

Of the thirty scheduled concerts in 1930, only two were canceled because of inclement weather. On one occasion, Arthur told a drenched audience, "If you stay, we'll play!" They did, and he conducted to a wildly cheering crowd of less than five hundred, huddled tightly against the stage. Another outdoor hazard was airplane noises, which became so intolerable that we finally asked the Logan Airport personnel to do something. An understanding management agreed to reroute airplane traffic during the hours of the concerts so planes would not fly directly over the Esplanade. However, it never prevented a music-loving private pilot from occasionally buzzing the Esplanade — especially during the soft, slower movements. Sometimes the noise level was so impossible we simply stopped playing until the flyer grew weary of the game. One night during an election campaign a blimp suddenly appeared overhead advertising John Volpe for Governor and Edward Brooke for Attorney General of Massachusetts. A scathing letter was written to both candidates, and we received an abject apology. Another evening, while I was conducting a slow movement of a Beethoven symphony, the Goodyear blimp suddenly appeared. We stopped the concert and waited for the flashing lights and noise to disappear. Then I went to the microphone and asked the huge audience to boycott the product and write the advertiser a protest letter. The incident received national attention; I felt I would surely be sued by the Goodyear Company, but I was fully vindicated when a telegram arrived from Akron, Ohio, closely followed by a letter of apology from the president of the corporation.

A visitor to the Esplanade cannot help but be impressed by the cosmopolitan audience that assembles each evening: Back Bay society drives up in chauffeur-driven limousines. Families arrive by subway. Taxis parade to the Charles River, quickly discharge their fares, then turn around for another trip. Hundreds of people anchor their boats in the Charles River. College students walk, or if their school (of the sixty-three universities in the metropolitan area of Boston) is too far away, they bicycle in clusters of twos and threes. Parking is at a premium; consequently, people arrive very early for the concert and make a night's party of it. People from every walk of life gather to listen and appreciate, eat everything from popcorn to seven-course meals, and sip enough wine to add a little romance.

An amusing newspaper item about the Esplanade appeared about thirty-five years ago. Arthur was conducting Beethoven's Eighth Symphony. The early summer night was balmy, the moon was full, and the gentlest of breezes caressed the audience. A group of well-dressed people from the North Shore decided to take in an Esplanade Concert. They arrived in their station wagon, spread out several blankets, and opened a flask. The music began. The talking and laughter of this group grew louder and louder. An elderly woman seated behind them with a red bandana wrapped about her head leaned forward, tapped a man on the shoulder, and said politely, "Excuse me, please. But you ain't supposed to talk when the damn music is playing. Shut up, or leave . . . thank you!"

Arthur treated his first audiences gingerly. He had no idea what the general populace liked in music, and he did not want them to run away. To assure success, he selected "Stars and Stripes Forever," several well-known operatic overtures he was positive the crowd knew by melody even if they did not know the names, Sigmund Romberg's brand new hit, "Blue Moon," and a lighter classical work. Little by little, Arthur began bringing in symphonies — one or two movements at a time — educating the masses to what he believed to be the better things in life. Then in 1935, he tested the orchestral taste of his audience by playing all the Beethoven symphonies, excepting the Ninth, which required a large chorus and soloists. The venture was a huge success. Since that time, the programs of the Esplanade have included some of the same music played by the BSO or any other symphony orchestra. Although serious in nature, the concerts were informal, unpretentious affairs, and even now there are no reserved seats, no enclosures, no ticket offices. No amount of money can save you a place on the grass. Everything is on a first-come, first-served basis. It was the way Arthur envisioned it and is precisely the way the Esplanade remains.

* * *

The Esplanade Concerts have, over the years, provided promising young players with their first performance as soloists with an orchestra. Some parents brought their children to the Esplanade Concert and pulled at Arthur's coattails after the concert to tell of their offsprings' talent. In some cases, he auditioned the child and, if the child proved to be talented, Arthur would allow him or her to play a concerto with the orchestra.

An important adjunct of the Esplanade concerts was, and still is, the series of Children's Concerts. Concerts usually begin on the Wednesday after the season's premiere performance. The time is always 10:15 in the morning. For several hours before the concert begins, the children come by foot, automobile, elevated trains, and buses, from as far away as Salem, Framingham, and Brockton, Massachusetts. It never takes long for the gigantic lawn facing Hatch Memorial Shell to fill with children of all ages. Arthur began the Children's Esplanade Concerts in 1938, and they have presented over the years talented soloists who have since become mature artists.

"Esplanade concerts in the evening were too late for the kids to be out," he recalled to a reporter. "To satisfy their musical enthusiasm, I decided to have short concerts aimed at and played solely for the children themselves. What nicer place than out-of-doors on a summer morning, where they can relax on the grass and simply enjoy themselves with music for fun? I purposely didn't make them an educational affair. Little folks love music which tells a story. They also respond quite nicely to lilting rhythms like a Strauss waltz or "Pomp and Circumstance." Martial music also gets a big hand, too, like Mozart's "Turkish March" and many of the Sousa pieces. Of course, the popular music from the movies and shows always creates a sensation, like the old favorites from Walt Disney's *Snow White and the Seven Dwarfs*. They even break out singing the words sometimes . . ."

The first Children's Esplanade Concert contained the type of varied program that has continued to be popular ever since: "Pomp and Circumstance," "The Mosquito Dance," "In the Hall of the Mountain King" from Grieg's *Peer Gynt Suite*, Handel's "Largo," as a violin solo, and "The Stars and Stripes Forever." The second and third concerts followed on consecutive weeks. When it became obvious that Friday was a difficult day for the parents, since it began the weekend, the concerts were switched to midweek, usually Wednesdays. An average attendance is something more than five thousand, but twice that number is not unusual. Every so often, especially when we do Prokofiev's *Peter and the Wolf*, as many as fifteen thousand children attend.

The Children's Concerts were, in some cases, steppingstones in the careers of future artists, many of whom have gone on to become a part of our American musical scene, either as recitalists or as members of major orchestras.

In 1968 I introduced a 14-year-old violinist, Peter Zazofsky, at one of the Children's Concerts. Peter, whose father, George, was also a fine violinist in the Boston Symphony, played the first movement of Mozart's Violin Concerto no. 4. That evening George Zazofsky was scheduled to perform the same concerto, but unfortunately, just before the concert he suffered an accident to his finger. Young Peter was hastily summoned, and performed the entire concerto in his father's place. I wonder how many times musical history has recorded the substitution of a son for his father. Peter Zazofsky, now a seasoned artist, has won a number of prestigious international competitions since that time, and recently appeared as soloist with the Boston Symphony Orchestra.

We have in the United States a wealth of talent among our young people, and it is to Arthur Fiedler's everlasting credit that he provided the opportunity for them to be heard, not only at the Esplanade concerts but at the Pops as well. A few names come to mind, like violinist Charles Castleman, who, at the age of four, knew all the Beethoven symphonies; young violinist Lynn Chang, with his astonishing technical ability at the age of eight; and pianist Fred Moyer, who, at ten years of age, astonished us with his playing of a Bach concerto. All of these players, and many more, are now pursuing successful careers in music.

*　　*　　*

The Esplanade audience begins arriving around 5:30 in the evening. Dots of green grass to the south of the Hatch Memorial Shell quickly disappear beneath chairs, blankets, and baby carriages as literally thousands stake out listening posts for the night's performance. In later years, when no more land was available around the shell, the audience swelled onto the Arthur Fiedler Bridge, which spans Storrow Memorial Drive. The Fiedler foot bridge, erected and dedicated in the summer of 1953 to celebrate Arthur's twenty-fifth season on the Esplanade, bears a plaque in honor of the man who "has here brought music of the masters to countless thousands in these concerts."

Arthur had a reputation around Boston as something of a rain god. The legend began one evening in 1949 during an Esplanade performance, when a storm wave threatened the concert. Turning and looking up toward the dark sky, Arthur lifted his baton, motioning the black clouds away. The sky suddenly brightened. At about ten o'clock, as the concert was concluding, there was a terrific clap of thunder. The orchestra sheltered their instruments and people ran for home. Since that time, people would stop Arthur on the street during Esplanade season and inquire about the weather. He would answer, "It's not going to rain," and he was invariably right. Not many performances over the years have been canceled because of bad weather — although one concert was almost stopped due to an extortion threat made against Arthur and his entire family.

In early July of 1934, Arthur began receiving a series of nasty letters. He attributed them to a crank. People in the spotlight often receive hate mail of one sort or another, so Arthur ignored them. One letter threatened Arthur with a severe beating. Another told him he would be thrown in the Charles River. What convinced Arthur that this was the work of a crackpot were threats against his wife, children, and family — in 1934 Arthur was a bachelor, and his entire immediate family, with the exception of his uncles Benny and Gustave and cousin Joe Zimbler, were all residing in Berlin, Germany. The writer of the letters was very angry at Arthur for refusing permission for the Esplanade shell to be used by the Greater Boston Emergency Relief Administration Chorus until after he completed his summer series of concerts. Arthur scoffed at the threats, but the Boston Symphony took an entirely different view of the situation and did not find any part of it amusing. The Boston and Metropolitan District Commission were called to plan protection. On the night of July 27, 1934, an armed detachment of police and several undercover officers combed the Esplanade for any signs of potential danger from a crowd estimated at over ten thousand. When after a week of constant surveillance Arthur could tolerate this invasion of his privacy no longer, the police withdrew, although Inspector John Manning acted as Arthur's bodyguard until the season ended.

Despite the donations of the Boston business community and the contribution boxes scattered throughout the Esplanade, the concerts were always in financial trouble. Arthur was the first to admit that he used all his acquaintances quite shamelessly to further the financial cause of the Esplanade, and he once solicited a large amount of money from the Italian Consul-General in Boston by conducting an all-Italian program. Another time, Arthur raised a few dollars by telegraphing music. Originating in the Western Union office on Congress Street, Arthur sat at a specially constructed keyboard and played a series of notes, which were then transmitted a thousand miles away to the J. C. Deagan carillon at the Chicago World's Fair. He played "America" on the keyboard attached to a Western Union telegraph typewriter. It was sent by electric signal at 10:15, the night of August 12, 1934, and operated the twenty-five-bell carillon heard by thousands of World Fair visitors. At two o'clock the following morning, the notes were broadcast across the country as a sign-off feature of the Columbia Broadcasting System, and a small fee was paid for the performance. That telemusicon was the first of its type ever used successfully anywhere in the world. Whether or not the broadcast notes came out in tune, Arthur never knew.

In 1938, the BSO took the Esplanade concerts under its wing, and Arthur's financial worries were over.

Arthur rarely relinquished the baton in the early days of the Esplanade; however, he did surrender it one evening to Charlie O'Connell, after being told by several people that the acoustics still left something to be desired, and he went out to listen. It was several years before the construction of the Hatch Memorial Shell, and Arthur decided to find out for himself just how bad the echo really was. Charlie O'Connell conducted the concert that night while Arthur roamed the Esplanade, listening to the tonal quality of the orchestra throughout the evening. No one recognized him or his eccentric behavior. Informality is the custom of the Esplanade, so when he began climbing up and over obstacles, roamed to the water's edge, or turned his back to the music, no one paid him the slightest attention. He returned to the shell after the concert, announced that the fifty instruments could be heard perfectly, and was convinced that the acoustics were adequate.

"It was a hell of a fight for survival," Arthur told a Boston *Post* reporter on the eve of his tenth anniversary at the Esplanade. "We didn't know from one day to the next if we could make it or not. Without the radio broadcasts and you people, the collection boxes would've probably remained empty. And the money's still tight. If it wasn't, I wouldn't be talking to you now. Next year, we build a permanent shell. I couldn't be happier. But what do we use to maintain it? I'm lousy with a hammer and nails."

*　　*　　*

When Constance Babcock, an indefatigable do-gooder and promoter of social betterment in the city of Boston, decided to organize a charity concert in Symphony Hall to benefit the Boston Dispensary and the Boston Floating Hospital, she decided no one was better qualified to assist her than Arthur Fiedler. She wanted him to conduct a Pops concert entitled *Music on the Riviera*. Arthur thought it was a splendid idea — especially the Riviera part, because it might remind people of the Charles River and the Esplanade.

Driving a sandwich truck through the streets of Boston, with members of the Junior League and the Vincent Club selling everything the vehicle carried, Arthur became an uncharacteristic huckster, talking up the forthcoming charity Pops concert and the need for funding for the next season's Esplanade. Constance Babcock got what she wanted — a sellout on both the concert and the sandwich truck, raising over fifteen hundred dollars for the hospitals, but Arthur did much better. The Esplanade Concert Fund got richer by two thousand dollars, and when the season opened the following July, not only did he have a new shell, but a little extra money to maintain it.

The Hatch Shell was the result of a conversation between Arthur and Attorney General Paul A. Dever (who later became governor of Massachusetts). Maria E. Hatch and her sister Lucy were proper Bostonians of inherited wealth. Neither ever married, and they died in 1926, thirteen days apart. In her will, Maria had left a quarter of a million dollars to be used to create a memorial to their brother Edward, who had died in 1910 and had been an ardent music lover and regular subscriber to the Boston Symphony. When Arthur was told the background of the Hatch family he enthusiastically convinced Dever that a music shell on the Esplanade would be a most appropriate memorial. Dever agreed, and the Edward Hatch Memorial Shell was built and dedicated in the summer of 1939, the tenth anniversary of the Esplanade Concerts.

"It's all been very exciting over the years," Arthur once told Ellen, "although I must say certain nights stick out in my memory. One in particular was August 15, 1945. That night we had over forty thousand people here at the Esplanade for a special Victory Program. Japan had surrendered the day before. I must have gotten a dozen letters afterward, telling me they met their future husbands or wives at that concert. They had come to the concert for the first time. It was the biggest day of their lives. We were finally at peace. Fantastic night, really!"

Another unusual night occurred on the evening of July 20, 1936. A musician famous at the turn of the century returned that night to play under the baton of his son. Emanuel Fiedler, now very old but still ramrod straight, once more took up his violin and bow. Never before had the elder Mr. Fiedler played under the direction of his son. What brought them together was a casual invitation from Arthur. The family had returned from Berlin to Boston for a visit, ostensibly to see Arthur conduct at the Esplanade. When Arthur extended the invitation, Emanuel accepted and played an entire concert.

*   *   *

The greatest Esplanade night by far, however, was in 1976, the Bicentennial year, when Arthur's Fourth of July concert took on a special meaning. A large audience was expected, but no one could have foreseen the size of the crowd that night. Even the night before the concert people began taking places on the grass in front of the Shell, staking out their claims with folding chairs and blankets. By six o'clock on the evening of the concert, Storrow Drive and all surrounding streets had to be closed to traffic as they became swollen with humanity. The open space in front of the Shell had long been filled, and now the crowds kept spilling over toward the sides and backward along the banks of the Charles River. By the time Fiedler arrived, via special police car, to begin the concert at 8:30, he was greeted by an estimated 400,000 people, undoubtedly the largest concert audience in history. Of course Arthur was moved, but the only comment he made as he arrived was, "Where the hell did they all come from!" Before going on stage that night he took an extra-long draft of his favorite bourbon.

The concert ended with the "1812" Overture of Tchaikovsky with cannon, church bells, and fireworks, followed by the inevitable "Stars and Stripes." I was excused from playing in the orchestra that night and took my place on the roof of a nearby building with remote controls, TV cameras, police crowd controllers, and scores of radio and TV announcers. At a little peninsula on the bank of the Charles River, soldiers of the 5th Battalion of the 187th Artillery of the Army Reserve, equipped with eight 105mm howitzers, were ready to fire intermittently at the precise moments indicated in the score by Tchaikovsky. The Church of the Advent stood ready with bell ringers to sound their amplified bells at the appropriate time, as also indicated by the composer; and to add to the excitement (although not prescribed by Tchaikovsky) a barge out on the river was ready to send up fireworks at the conclusion of the overture. All of these forces were coordinated by electronic communication from the roof of the building, and it was one of those Cecil B. DeMille productions that had to be done on the first "take," with no margin for error.

One could say that the height of Arthur Fiedler's career was reached at this concert, when, in addition to the nearly half million people who lined the banks of the Charles, countless millions heard the concert over radio and TV. That night I began to realize the enormous appeal of this man and his contribution to the popular culture of the world. As he was escorted by a cordon of police, after the concert, to his waiting car, with shouts of "Hi, Arthur!" ringing in his ears, he must have felt a sense of exhilaration; yet he never showed it. A more introspective person might have realized what he meant to the masses, a figure of identification with them, a hero who had "made it," yet was still one of them, a man of the people.

*   *   *

During his 1976 Boston Summerthing program, Mayor Kevin White suggested the Pops play a series of park concerts. Arthur objected. "The people can all come to the Esplanade," he said. So I agreed to conduct the five free concerts in various parks throughout the city. Arthur seemed vindicated when the orchestra was stoned by unruly youths one night in Franklin Park, and we were forced to cancel the concert midway through the performance.

*   *   *

Although the 1976 Esplanade Concert was the climax of Arthur's career, the 1978 concert, celebrating his incredible fiftieth consecutive year of conducting the Esplanade Concerts, turned out to be his last. This concert was also a gala one, if somewhat smaller in attendance. This time perhaps a hundred thousand people were in attendance, most of them wearing buttons reading "Fiedler's 50th 4th." Again there was the "1812" Overture with cannon, bells, and fireworks, followed by Sousa's "Stars and Stripes Forever," also with accompanying fireworks.

By this time Arthur was in his 84th year, and although he had begun to fail visibly, there was still an unbelievable vitality in his conducting, even though he had to be assisted in getting on and off the podium.

During the intermission there were speeches of praise from the governor, the mayor, and other dignitaries; and Arthur was presented with a gigantic leather-bound volume of signatures and congratulatory messages from the citizens of Greater Boston. For weeks before the concert, this volume had been on display at the City Hall, the Public Library, the State House, and supermarkets, where people had lined up to inscribe their names and good wishes.

Again he left the grounds after the concert, surrounded by police and shouts of "Hi, Arthur!" from the crowds. The world's greatest concert and the world's second greatest concert, both noted in the Guinness *Book of World Records*, were now history, but a tradition had been established that will probably continue for many years.

(V)

The Maestro

I F ARTHUR HAD ONE GENIUS IN LIFE, it was his uncanny ability to create balanced programs. No matter what the person's musical tastes, Arthur touched him at one time or another. Instinctively, he knew what people wanted. He was fascinated by every spectrum of music and constructed programs accordingly. To understand Arthur's program-making skill is to appreciate his mania for detail. He continually questioned what people wanted to hear. He frequently called his arranger, Richard Hayman, in New York, to ask what was popular at the moment.

It is a tribute to Arthur's catholic tastes and his fanatical desire to satisfy the widest possible public preferences that he included in his programs music of many diversified styles: light and heavy classics, the popular standards of today, hits from musical plays and comedies, established concert pieces, and a variety of novelties presented first to the Boston audience, then — via radio and television — to the entire world. Arthur was shrewd in combining the familiar with the new. He would sit at his desk for hours, juggling the contents of a program. I have seen him discard a piece at the last minute, inserting a more suitable offering in keeping with the evening's audience. More amazing still was the fact that Arthur's instincts were always accurate. No matter where he conducted in the world, this ability was invariably the same. He may not have been able to speak the language of the orchestra he was conducting, or the people in the audience, but he was most assuredly able to satisfy their musical desires.

In the early years, the most potent single force involved with the program-making decisions of each concert was Leslie Rogers, the librarian of the Boston Symphony Orchestra. Rogers was a small man, with gray hair, penetrating blue eyes, and an astutely quiet nature. He had been in the Symphony since the First World War. Possessing a phenomenal memory, Leslie was totally consumed by his job. The library was his fortress. No cross-index file ever needed to be consulted. Without blinking, he could tell you what piece was played when, who wrote it, how many musicians were involved, the score number, and the entire history of the work as it applied to the BSO. To question his memory was an exercise in futility. He was never wrong — not once in the entire time I knew him from 1938 until his death from pneumonia during a BSO European tour twenty-five years ago.

During the early days of the Pops, the orchestra was non-union, and Leslie also acted as personnel manager. Arthur, at the time, had a desk in the library facing Rogers. We would sit there for hours making programs. When Leslie or I would suggest a piece of music, Arthur would automatically turn it down. Twenty minutes later, he would suggest the same piece and we would nod approval. Leslie never became excited. No matter how much Arthur complained, Rogers remained calm. He knew Arthur would come around to his way of thinking before the session ended. I particularly enjoyed watching the interplay between the two men. Rogers knew he could always lead Arthur to water, but could never make him drink. To save time he occasionally turned the liquid to Old Fitzgerald. Leslie was given to telling long, drawn-out stories. For the most part, they were not particularly funny, and Arthur would bellow: "Start in the middle!"

After Leslie Rogers died, Leonard Burkat, musical advisor to Charles Munch when he was the Boston Symphony conductor, joined our program-making sessions. As usual, we would all sit in the library discussing one program or another. Burkat enjoyed the same luck that Leslie did. Arthur shouted down every suggestion; however, when Leonard left the Boston Symphony Orchestra to become a vice-president of Columbia Records, Arthur would look at all of us with dour frustration and demand, "Why can't you make suggestions like Burkat?" Even though we were there to help him, Arthur innately distrusted us, and the final decision had to be his. I have often wondered how Arthur achieved this program-making ability, which I still try to emulate.

After attending a Boston Celtics basketball game where the National Anthem was played before the game, Arthur decided against playing it at the beginning of Esplanade Concerts; it would be too much like a sporting event. To lend more importance to the piece, he decided to play it at the beginning of the second part of the concert. Now there would be no feeling of "getting it over with," and the entire audience would be present. The National Anthem was not played at regular Pops concerts, except when it was preceded by the anthem of a foreign country.

*   *   *

With few exceptions, each night at the Pops throughout the season is sponsored by various organizations. Their names appear on the program as "among those present." These include women's clubs, the Junior League, fraternity and sorority groups, ethnic orders, high school and college clubs, industrial trade unions, and many others. Some nights are traditionally given over to only one specific organization — such as a Harvard twenty-fifth class reunion, the New England Conservatory, the Eire Society, Tufts or Boston universities. For every Harvard

Arthur on his tenth birthday, in 1904

Johanna Fiedler, Arthur's mother, and his eldest sister, Fredericka, in 1892

Emanuel Fiedler, Arthur's father, in a photograph taken the year Arthur was born, 1894

Arthur and his father on holiday at a Baltic Sea resort in 1922

Both Arthur (right) and Emanuel Fiedler (left) played in the
Berliner Streich-Quartet during the years Arthur was studying
at the Royal Academy of Music in Berlin

The Sinfonietta in 1924. Arthur is the conductor (at center),
and his Uncle Benny is seated at his left

Emanuel and Arthur Fiedler standing at the stage entrance to
Symphony Hall in Boston on May 7, 1936

Arthur during a visit to Fiedler, Pennsylvania,
in September 1932

Arthur as an apprentice seaman in the United States
Coast Guard Temporary Reserve. He had enlisted
in 1943 at almost 49 years of age

At the piano with son, Peter, in 1952

Ellen and Arthur Fiedler with a
family scrapbook

Practicing with his daughters,
Johanna (Yummie), left, and Debbie

Trumpeter Al Hirt protects his ears from Arthur's blast in October 1964,
during Fiedler's visit to New Orleans to conduct Hirt's band

Arthur and Harry Dickson making program selections in the
library at Symphony Hall

Arthur at the wheel of the 1937 Ford fire engine given to him
by his family for his 75th birthday

Danny Kaye and Harry Ellis Dickson admire a poster outside
Symphony Hall, 1971

Arthur with one of his favorite pets, Sparkie, in 1972

Boston's mayor, Kevin White, left, with Arthur and Boston Symphony
Orchestra conductor Seiji Ozawa at Symphony Hall, in 1973

Maestro Fiedler in performance

With Joan Kennedy at Tanglewood, in 1976, going over the score for
The Young Person's Guide to the Orchestra, which Mrs. Kennedy narrated

Arthur and Ellen Fiedler with Ray Bolger, who appeared with the
Pops in May 1976

Arthur at the barre with young ballerinas in preparation for
the annual Boston Ballet performance of Tchaikovsky's
Nutcracker Suite, in 1974

An audience view of Arthur preceding an *Evening at Pops*
broadcast, in 1974

A celebration of Arthur's 80th birthday at City Hall
in Boston, December 1974

Crowds gathering for the Bicentennial Concert
on the Esplanade, July 4, 1976

A relaxed moment

The annual Pops Christmas concert, 1977

Listening to the playbacks from a 1978 recording session

Ellen Fiedler during a performance of Copland's *Lincoln Portrait* with the Boston Pops Touring Orchestra

Arthur the night he welcomed home the Boston Symphony Orchestra from its momentous trip to China, March 20, 1979

reunion, the group would buy out Symphony Hall. Drinks and dinner were served before the concert, and everyone was tipsy by eight. One year, an alumnus insisted on buying champagne for the entire orchestra.

"I wonder how that guy's going to feel tomorrow when he gets the bill," Arthur said to me.

Whenever possible, Arthur tried to honor the requests of the various organizations, including their chosen soloists. Auditions were held ahead of time and the would-be soloists were either accepted or rejected. Sometimes his judgment faltered and a soloist was allowed to play who was not quite ready. One such incident that comes to mind involved an evening that was taken over by the Christian Science Church. They proposed an unknown pianist and were adamantly unwilling to change their request. Arthur had grave reservations concerning her ability, but agreed after management again pointed out the number of tickets the group had purchased. He allowed her to play her chosen work, the Variations of César Franck.

I was new to the orchestra. At my first rehearsal, Benny, who by this time had already spent thirty-five years in the orchestra, gave me some hurried instructions: "Take it easy," he advised. "You don't have to work that hard! That's not Koussevitzky, it's only Arthur!" He was really proud of his nephew, and although he, himself, constantly disparaged him, would defend him fiercely if others did.

"I greet all my friends in the Hall." He smiled wistfully. "But sometimes when I lose my place, I will say, 'Bixen, Bixen,' and you should point to the place with your bow." (He never referred to anyone by his right name.)

On the night of the aforementioned concert with the not-really-ready soloist, no sooner had she started than she got hopelessly lost. She began to flounder, finally picking up the music after skipping thirty bars. Arthur somehow found her and quickly brought us together. However, it did not last very long; she immediately lost her place again. Each time we would try to pick up the pieces by hoping to discover precisely where she was in her meanderings. All the while, Uncle Benny was glaring at me, shouting over and over again:

"Bixen! Bixen!"

I looked at him and shrugged. He was expecting me to show him where we were, but by this time I was as hopelessly lost as the pianist, the orchestra, and Arthur. When I did not help him find the correct place, Benny got furious. The piece finally ended. Her friends gave the soloist a standing ovation, but Uncle Benny would not talk to me for the remainder of the evening.

Perhaps the single most popular evening was, and still is, the annual Old Timers' Night, traditionally sold out well in advance. The program always consisted of old favorites and song medleys in which the audience was invited to sing along. These programs — like all others — were made with painstaking care about three weeks in advance, in meetings that were attended by the BSO's librarians, Arthur's secretary, Fiedler, and me.

"The Pops concerts are a good melting pot of music," he once told an interviewer. "I guess we're the classiest jukebox in the world." Arthur knew that popular music had an immediate appeal, but he insisted on playing classical music, too. The amalgamation of the two was what made the Pops unique. Arthur's classical background enabled him to select pieces that would please the audience and subtly educate them, as well.

"I am not and never have been a man to carry a flag and lead great masses of people to great music," he said once. "My aim is to give them a good time, an evening's entertainment."

Each year, Richard Hayman, our arranger, would come up with some novelty that would become the *hit* of that season. It was played almost every night, either on the program or as an encore. When the film *Jaws* appeared — with music composed by John Williams — and became a success in movie houses throughout the world, Hayman made an arrangement of the theme music. At the first performance an inflated rubber shark appeared over the heads of the percussion players, who then shoved it toward Arthur. Without missing a beat, Arthur would automatically whack the shark back to the percussion players. The music was well received, and the shark was an instant success with the audience. People, as we suspected they would, began to request it every night.

Who can forget the Davy Crockett craze, when Arthur would wear a coonskin cap during the performance? It all seems ludicrous now, but then the audience loved it, and Fiedler obliged. During the Beatles phenomenon in the sixties, Arthur asked Richard Hayman to make a Pops arrangement of a piece called "I Want to Hold Your Hand." This, too, became the hit of the season. Arthur was severely criticized by the musical snobs but, as always, paid no attention to them. Each time we played the tune he would don a Beatle wig, creating even more sensation and disapproval from proper Bostonians everywhere. When we first rehearsed the Paul McCartney–John Lennon song, we discovered directions for which none of us had ever been trained. At one place in the music, we violinists were to put our instruments in our laps and clap our hands. At another time, we were to stop playing and sing "la-la-la." Eugene Lehner, our Hungarian-born, European-trained violist and former member of the internationally known Kolisch String Quartet, as well as a personal friend of Arnold Schoenberg, refused to either clap his hands or sing. "In my conservatory," he said disdainfully, "they did not teach me those things!"

Esplanade programs were always more serious in nature than Pops programs. Although Arthur later added popular music to the latter part of the program, he conceived the Esplanade as a summer continuation of the Boston Symphony Concerts, and usually each program contained a serious overture and a classical symphony. His basic intention was to show that serious music could be played out-of-doors. He also satisfied his own desire to conduct the music in which he had been nurtured.

One time [as Laning Humphrey, the Boston Sunday *Post* feature writer who was to become Fiedler's publicist and the Pops archivist, remembered], Arthur decided to introduce the large mobs of people on the Esplanade to more substantial music, but gradually — two movements of a four-movement symphony on one program and the remaining two movements the following night. I questioned whether it was advisable. "Playing Brahms is always smart," he said. "Besides, it will be good for them and good for us." The outdoor acoustics made the piccolo and bass drum too conspicuous. I was going to mention this to him after the concert, but before I could open my mouth, Arthur cornered me, and said, "Lousy, wasn't it?"

Beginning in January 1951, when Arthur inaugurated a series of Monday evening Pops broadcasts over NBC radio coast to coast, he presented a number of first performances of music new even to his Boston audience. Among them were the Khachaturian Piano Concerto, the Poulenc Organ Concerto, the Bizet Symphony in C, and the Overture to Berlioz's *Beatrice and Benedict*.

The Pops public knew precisely what to expect, and Arthur gave them what they wanted. By letters, post cards, telegrams, and telephone, the audience has over the years aimed a literal bombardment of requests at Arthur and the Boston Pops. If it was humanly possible and fit within the framework of the Pops program, Arthur generally gave the people what they wanted.

The leading favorites of the audience are those with loud endings. Pieces like the *William Tell* Overture, Tchaikovsky's "1812" Overture, the introduction to Act III of *Lohengrin,* the march "Pomp and Circumstance," and Ravel's *Bolero* are all big favorites and end fortissimo. On the other hand, Arthur always balanced his programs with other, less dramatic pieces, like Handel's "Largo," a Strauss waltz, or Mascagni's Intermezzo from *Cavalleria Rusticana.* For a time, we were playing George Gershwin's *Rhapsody in Blue* so often we began to hate it — especially Patsy Cardillo, who despised his opening clarinet cadenza.

Arthur saved all his prepared encores for the last section of the program. The audience took them to be surprises, but a sign was placed against the backstage wall by Joe Spotts, the Symphony valet, and it displayed the name of the piece to be played. Arthur never played an encore that was not planned for that evening, because the music from the library had to be placed in the musicians' folders ahead of time. He also disregarded any audience requests handed up to him through the musicians. He once said, "Someone in the audience is always having a birthday, and we would be playing 'Happy Birthday' every night of the week."

In 1949, Arthur was invited to conduct the San Francisco Symphony, giving him an opportunity to try the Pops format in another city, and he accepted the challenge. Pierre Monteux, his old mentor, had been conducting the San Francisco Symphony Orchestra for over ten years. A series of broadcasts under the sponsorship of Standard Oil of California had been a Sunday evening programming phenomenon for a number of years. However, from the mail Monteux received, the *Standard Hour,* as it was called, was beginning to lose a portion of its audience to a new kind of music: big-band jazz. Arthur was the first to realize something must be done. He was scheduled to conduct a broadcast concert on April 17, 1950, at San Francisco's Civic Auditorium. Tickets were sold out several weeks in advance, and Standard Oil of California was advertising the concert with a substantial budget.

Arthur chose his program carefully. In honor of Pierre Monteux and his immense popularity in San Francisco, he resurrected a piece called "Rose Mousse," a tidbit by a composer named Bosc, because the Maestro had told Arthur that during Monteux's honeymoon he had picked a moss rose every morning to be placed on his bride's breakfast tray. The concert was a great success. Immediately after the conclusion of the broadcast, Joseph Dyer, executive secretary of the San Francisco Art Commission, approached Arthur about establishing an ongoing San Francisco Pops Festival the following year. It would begin in July, run six weeks, and be sponsored by Standard Oil of California, to be simulcast on radio as well as on experimental television, which was at that time gaining a strong foothold in the City by the Bay. Arthur agreed to terms, returned to Boston, and notified Symphony Hall that immediately following next year's Boston Pops season, he would be conducting in San Francisco.

This, of course, presented a series of logistical problems. First, what to do about the Esplanade? Second, when to begin rehearsal in San Francisco so that a half-summer of programming could be accomplished without its lapsing over into his other tour commitments? Finally, could a six-nights-a-week series be done over six weeks in San Francisco as it was done for ten weeks each year in Boston?

The bulk of Monteux's San Francisco Orchestra jumped at the opportunity to make extra money during the summer as the Boston Symphony personnel had been doing for years, but the possibility of doing six concerts per week on the West Coast was impractical. Standard Oil of California would finance only one per week, with two extras. Thus, Arthur would conduct a total of only eight concerts in the summer of 1951. By carefully juggling his schedule, Arthur could fly back and forth for the Esplanade Concerts — at least for that season — and the free outdoor series would not be disturbed. (Four years later, when Arthur became too involved with San Francisco, I began conducting the Esplanade Concerts and continued to do so every year thereafter. Only on the Fourth of July each summer did Arthur return to conduct.) Also answered was the rehearsal problem. By doing only eight concerts, there was plenty of time to rehearse the San Francisco Orchestra and prepare programs.

During planning sessions Arthur told the management in San Francisco, "You're liable to have a number of fights if you sell whiskey to the audience." (Boston Pops audiences have never been served anything stronger than wine or beer.)

"We'll have worse fights in our town if we don't," he was told.

The first season opened to a Civic Auditorium crowd of less than one-third capacity. Arthur was mortified. He wanted to cancel and go home. Then the second week, the audience filled a little more than half the seats. Arthur felt only slightly better about the situation. Determined to work harder than ever, Arthur made himself available for every interview requested. The third concert drew two thirds of a full house. At the last concert in the series more than five thousand came, which still was not capacity. Arthur returned to Boston less than jubilant. He had drawn twenty-four thousand people for eight concerts, which seemed incredible to the San Francisco hierarchy. However, capacity was twice that amount, and Arthur was accustomed to playing before full houses and was determined to do something about the obvious lack of interest displayed by the San Francisco populace.

A tremendous television and billboard campaign was launched, and the following year the attendance nearly doubled. By 1960, the attendance situation had turned around. Season subscribers had their tickets for the following year twelve months in advance. Seats were left to relatives in wills. A couple fought out a divorce settlement before a San Francisco Superior Judge over who had rights to the Pops Festival tickets. Scalpers were demanding a fortune in the lobby of every hotel in town. Between the conventioneers and the tourists, they did a brisk business for the precious Pops seats, asking as much as fifty dollars a ticket — and getting it easily. The fire marshal told the management of the Civic Auditorium there could be no standing room. People screamed for his head. Arthur sided with the fire department, and was made honorary chief.

*   *   *

In May of 1938, Arthur and the Pops presented, for the first and only time, an entire ballet, with dancers, costumes, and simple scenery. It was the premier performance of a new ballet, *The Incredible Flutist* by Walter Piston. The entire stage was taken over by the dancers, and the orchestra played from illuminated music stands on the floor. It was an unusual, gala affair, with the composer present, and received wide and enthusiastic press coverage. The choreography was conceived by a local ballet master, Jan Veen, who danced the leading role.

Until the early seventies, when Arthur began to conduct the Boston Ballet's annual Christmas performances of *The Nutcracker,* this was the only experience Arthur had had with the ballet. Arthur Fiedler's *Nutcracker* became part of Boston's Christmas tradition, and he would conduct some fifteen consecutive performances each December, one of them always on December 17, his birthday. After one of these performances, he would come onto the stage for a bow, and a huge birthday cake would be wheeled out while the audience sang "Happy Birthday."

*   *   *

In 1975, the biggest New Year's Eve party in Boston occurred at Symphony Hall. New York may have had Guy Lombardo, but we had Arthur Fiedler. He pushed Bobby Orr and the Boston Bruins' hockey team right off the front page of every newspaper in town. The concert did not begin until ten o'clock, but for two hours beforehand the capacity audience rang out the old year on all three levels of Symphony Hall. Under the marble eyes of the balcony statues where Bacchus reigned, Myron Romanul played Scott Joplin. The Empire Brass Quintet entertained in the Cabot-Cahners Room, spilling over into the Hatch Memorial Room downstairs, and the WUZ — the orchestra's jazz combo — occupied the main level, where the seats had been removed to make way for tables and a small dance floor. Signs on the second level advertised a fund-raising auction: "A Trustee will doodle your request, minimum bid $40." Visitors wearing cardboard hats supplied by Symphony Hall talked, danced, and drank champagne. I introduced the concert, announcing that the program would reveal the dual personalities of the Boston Symphony Orchestra.

For the first half, Arthur and the orchestra appeared in white tie and tails and played a rather serious program. By the second half, we had changed into our regular Pops blue coats and black ties, with Arthur in his red coat. The overture to *Die Fleder-maus* received the most enthusiastic applause. At the first notes of Strauss's most famous waltz, couples poured onto the dance floor — a dream fulfilled for anyone who had ever wished to dance to a Viennese waltz. Then brilliant lights illuminated the entire Hall so that the remainder of the program could be tele-vised throughout the world.

During the intermission, Arthur had his usual nip of bourbon in the Green Room, was asked several questions by invited guests, and surprised us all by giving a straight answer to a woman who wondered how to interest her small children in music.

"I can only tell you what I did with my three," Arthur began, sitting back in his chair and looking over at Ellen as if silently asking for support. "I gave them a little record player of their own when they were very young and permitted them to play what they liked. When they began to show obvious interest, I started them at the piano, taking lessons from a teacher con-nected with the orchestra. But you must remember, it is essential that they practice. Most rebel against it. I know I certainly did. But you must keep at them — relentlessly, if necessary. They don't like to brush their teeth, but they do it — or should — at least twice a day."

Ellen and I exchanged glances. Arthur did not know the first thing about his children, and couldn't have cared less. Once during an interview, he was asked about Yummie, Debbie, and Peter. What were they currently doing with their lives? Arthur thought Yummie was working as a librarian for the New York Philharmonic, when in fact she was in their publicity depart-ment. Debbie had graduated with honors from Harvard Law School and was with a firm in New York. Arthur had no idea of its name, its location, or how to contact his younger daughter if ever the need should arise. Peter was still playing rock 'n' roll, according to his father. The fact that at the time the boy was well into a career in television production was never mentioned. Arthur did not know that. His family was the least most important item on Arthur's agenda, but, as Ellen so often told me, they loved him in spite of his impossible disposition and his miserly habits.

Intermission ended. We returned to the stage. The television lights came up full. An enormous pink and green greeting card garland was draped across the back of the stage. Arthur came up the aisle to the podium, acknowledged the standing ovation, and began to conduct. The audience talked quietly, creating an undercurrent of New Year's Eve frivolity. We shifted to excerpts from Tchaikovsky's *Nutcracker*. Woytek Lowski and Laura Young of the Boston Ballet danced the pas de deux nicely, but the warmest ovation from the milling crowd came after the athletic choreography of the Trepak. The moment the dancers left the stage, Arthur flipped the page of his score, nodded once, and we struck up a lengthy medley of familiar dance tunes.

Again, hundreds of people surged onto the modest dance floor. Arthur thought they did so just to make a brief appearance on national television, but people don't spend an entire evening with a frozen smile on their faces, not even politicians running for re-election. People were dancing in the aisles, along the hallways, in the lobby — anywhere they might move their feet, wiggle their shoulders, and perspire beneath the television lights. Arthur turned to them and led an old-fashioned sing-along. He looked like a stout Mitch Miller, minus the goatee.

The clock over the stage ticked off the final seconds of the old year. Balloons fell from the ceiling. Whistles blew. Streamers flew through the air. Everyone cheered. They broke into song, undoubtedly the classiest rendition of "Auld Lang Syne" in all of Boston. The concert rang to a close. Arthur returned to the Green Room, mopping his face with a clean white towel. He poured himself a drink. Ellen joined him. We toasted long life and the New Year.

VI

An Introverted
Santa Claus

Arthur was the perfect stoic. I often thought he was a reincarnate of the Greek philosopher who founded the school of stoicism. By definition, he was seemingly indifferent to or unaffected by joy, grief, pleasure, or pain. He had no formal religious beliefs. Music was his religion, the score his bible.

Arthur had no sympathy for sickness, either in himself or in others. He actually suffered four heart attacks during his lifetime, and fooled the doctors every time. He never paid the slightest attention to their directions.

Arthur's history of coronary attacks dated from the forties. One Saturday evening during a concert, I noticed toward the last part of the program that Arthur's face had become ash-gray. He fumbled for his little pillbox in his left hand coat pocket, popped a nitroglycerine tablet into his mouth, and continued conducting. At the end, he barely made it to his dressing room. After only a few seconds' rest, he insisted on going back to the stage for a bow. Nothing anyone could say would dissuade him. He returned, slumped into a chair, squeezed his eyes tightly shut, and waited for the pain to ease. A short time later, Ellen and I helped him into his car, and she drove him home. About an hour later, I telephoned their house. Ellen had insisted on calling the doctor. Arthur was too weak to argue, even though the very mention of the word *doctor* was tantamount to waving a red flag under his nose. Dr. Samuel A. Levine came to the house and ordered Arthur to the hospital. Arthur was not leaving his quarters. After pleading and cajoling unsuccessfully, after threatening to withdraw as Arthur's physician, after hearing Arthur vehemently refuse hospitalization, Dr. Levine gave in — but not before a nurse and cardiograph machine were brought to the house.

The next day it was determined that this was Arthur's second heart attack. Even so, he adamantly refused to go to the hospital. He stayed in bed all day Sunday and actually returned to the podium the following evening to conduct a televised concert. Dr. Levine told his students at Harvard, "I turned on the television set and was amazed to see Arthur Fiedler walking toward the podium. I knew he was going to drop dead." Obviously, he did not. Indeed, Arthur became the nemesis of cardiologists everywhere. He was the classic example of what not to do and still beat the odds.

A few years later he suffered another heart attack, and this time he was hospitalized. The following appeared in the *New England Journal of Medicine* some time later:

In the early spring of 1944 a 50-year-old man was admitted to the Peter Bent Brigham Hospital because of a second myocardial infarction. The course was uneventful. After about two weeks of bed rest, his physician, Dr. Samuel A. Levine, told the intern to let the patient out of bed, begin ambulation, and discharge him during the following week. The astonished intern asked Dr. Levine why he was departing from the then usual practice of keeping such a patient hospitalized for six weeks.

Dr. Levine pointed out that the patient's professional career would be jeopardized if he were not able to begin work very soon. He added that his knowledge of what caused heart attacks and what factors promoted or inhibited recovery was at best uncertain. "If patients smoke, I tell them to stop. If they don't smoke, I suggest they start. I try to change some factor in their lives — but I'm certainly not sure that six weeks of rest is as important for this artist's future life as letting him get back to his work, even though that work is physically vigorous."

The patient was Arthur Fiedler.

Throughout his life Arthur experienced a number of other medical problems, which he tolerated with disdain. At one time, he developed a rash on both legs which would have driven lesser men mad. It must have been terribly annoying. He once yanked up his trouser leg to show me the horrifying result of his scratching. I suggested he see a dermatologist. "What the hell do they know?" he demanded, and waited patiently for the rash to heal.

Another time, he developed a severe case of bursitis in his right arm. He would enter Symphony Hall with his conducting arm in a sling, change into his rehearsal clothes, drop the sling on the table, and walk out on stage as if nothing was wrong. During the evening performance, he conducted with his customary vigor, then returned to the Green Room and replaced the sling. To Arthur, ailments — real or imaginary — were a definite sign of weakness, meant to be conquered. He could tolerate vulnerability neither in himself nor in others.

Despite his lack of sentimentality, the following appeared under Arthur's name in the Boston Sunday *Advertiser* a couple of days before Christmas, 1962:

In this happy and full life of mine many Christmases have been unforgettable — at any age, in many parts of the world, each for a different reason. And for me, Christmas has not always occurred only on December 25. I've had, sometimes, several Christmases in one year and at other times it has seemed several years between Christmases. From all of this there is one Christmas, which is perhaps the most real and unforgettable for me.

Yes, there it is, and it was Christmas, 1961.

I had been away to conduct a series of concerts in Chicago for television distribution. The work had gone well, but I couldn't complete the series before I had to return East for some pressing business. It was agreed that I would fly from Boston back to Chicago on December 23 to conduct the last program for the television cameras. All would have been uneventful — I actually enjoyed my thousands of miles in the air each year — had a blizzard not descended on Chicago at the same time I descended. But I did manage to get through the storm and to finish the last heavy work session by midafternoon of Christmas Eve. My spirits rose as my chauffeur skillfully but slowly navigated the snow-clogged and wonderfully decorated streets to the Chicago airport. I would be home in a few hours.

I knew something was wrong when I saw the nervous milling crowds at the airport. Alas! New England was now having a blizzard and no planes could fly to Boston. Christmas on a bench in the waiting room of an airport, albeit a beautiful and modern facility, would certainly be unforgettable but not to my liking. Suddenly those of us slouched wearily around the waiting room heard an announcement that one plane would attempt to leave for New England.

Stronghearted aboard!

I happily took the chance. We stopped in Cleveland to pick up other stranded souls, but the courageous pilot could promise us little for the rest of the trip — we might end up in Norfolk or Norway. The storm grew more intense and our plane was buffeted like the little old-fashioned doll in the glass sphere when you turn the globe upside-down and the snow falls.

We finally came over Boston. The city was obliterated by the storm. Just as the pilot announced we would have to turn south to an open airport, the heavens cleared — just momentarily — and the plane instantly changed course, dived downward, and slid through the snow to a bumpy stop. By the time I had stepped from the plane the heavens had closed again and the snow — now waist deep — swirled on.

As I forced my way through the howling night to the deserted terminal I heard a happy cry. It was my elder daughter — some claim she is the apple of my eye, but I really love each of my children one hundred per cent — who had somehow, quite miraculously, forced her little car through all the drifts to meet me and to take me home at this very late hour of Christmas Eve to my family and my fireplace.

This was my most unforgettable Christmas.

A lovely story, most certainly. I have no idea who wrote it.

If Arthur returned to Boston from Chicago in a blinding snowstorm, he would have been complaining all the way, and contemplating his next assignment, not Christmas at home with his family. If the Christmas lights shone bright on Hyslop Road, it was because of Ellen.

As with his Christmas story, the press and the public were delighted by the following interview that appeared in the Boston *Herald-Advertiser*:

SUNDAY, June 1, 1975. There is a motto I created about three years ago. Today it's plastered all over Symphony Hall. It goes, "He who rests, rots." That's become my slogan, the words I live by.

I've just celebrated my eightieth birthday, and I'm still going strong. Perhaps much too much so. But I like my work, and I think activity is the best thing in the world for you. If you're not active, you deteriorate. You might as well give up. People ask me, "When are you going to retire?" I'm not even thinking about retirement. Of course, you have to face nature. You must realize that the mind and the body are not as elastic as they once were. My profession, especially, can be very tiring and time-consuming.

Conducting is strenuous work, both physically and mentally. I worry like a mother hen about my chicks. I know all the treacherous things ahead, like a difficult passage for the trombone in the "Bolero," and I worry about it. I'm loaded down with correspondence, scores, recordings, tapes, travel, etc. Sometimes the repetition can be boring. The doctor who has done one thousand appendectomies probably doesn't find the thousand and first as exciting as the first one. And there are always little problems — sometimes in being guest conductor with other orchestras or with hotel and travel arrangements. It isn't all a bed of roses. But still, I find my work fascinating. There's a great sense of power, immediate power. When the conductor begins, BING! one hundred musicians must come down with you on a split second. Otherwise, you don't get any kind of decent performance. He who rests, rots. I know as a motto it's not very profound, but it fits me. I haven't rested much, but I'm not rotting yet. When I die, if I don't have my baton in my hand, I at least want to have my boots on. It might be a good epitaph for my tombstone except that I hope to be cremated.

There's one other very important phrase for me, one I learned very early in life. It came from my mother, who gave me my first music lessons. She was an amateur musician, a pianist. One day I was talking badly about a neighbor kid. She stopped me, and said, "You can never raise yourself by lowering someone else." Even then those words impressed me. It's so easy in any profession to say, "Oh, he's not so hot." But I try not to do that. To say that someone doesn't play the fiddle very well doesn't make you play the fiddle any better. I think of Jascha Heifetz, a great violinist and an immaculate performer. One time he had an off night, but just because this great man, from whom you'd expect perfection, was slightly off in one performance, many people were quick to say, "Ah haa! Heifetz is done, he's slipping." People seem to forget you cannot raise yourself in the estimation of others by talking someone else down. Give every man his due.

Despite these sentiments, in all the years I knew Arthur I cannot remember a conversation between us that was not filled with cynicism. As a perfectionist, he constantly found fault with everybody and everything. His friends had to accept him with a tolerance the rest of his audience did not require.

* * *

Arthur never refused a request. If he was available, he would appear with any and all kinds of orchestras, even high school bands. He had a sixth sense about publicity and was game for everything. He once spent an entire evening at a disco dance hall to raise money for an orphanage. Another time he conducted an all-Jewish symphony to raise emergency funding for Israel. He paid all his own expenses to and from New York, did not ask for or receive a fee, and returned without mentioning the trip to anyone.

If the word *friend* denotes an exchange of confidences between people, Arthur had no such friends. A few people were allowed to do things for him, among them, John Cahill. John spent a great deal of time in Arthur's company. He was a burly, good-natured Irishman, who made a career of helping people and being Arthur's friend. They met during the Second World War as reserves in the Coast Guard, which Arthur had joined after being turned down by the Army because of his age and for having flat feet. Arthur's tenure in the Coast Guard proved to be great publicity for both that branch of the armed services and himself; he was frequently photographed in uniform. Actually, he never sailed too far away from Boston Harbor and was a little frightened of the sea.

Cahill and Arthur became inseparable during their limited tour of duty. Their contrasting personalities made them an odd couple indeed; John, the glad-handing extrovert, and Arthur, the suspicious introvert. Cahill became a nightly backstage vis-

itor to the Pops, constantly escorting visitors there to meet Fiedler — a habit Arthur deplored and about which he complained
loudly, but to no avail. Cahill simply ignored him.

John Cahill was completely devoted to Arthur. He adored
the Arthur Fiedler image, the man envied by an ogling public.
Fiedler, the person, was as distant from him as he was from
everyone else. Cahill's relationship with Arthur's family was
much warmer and closer than with Arthur himself, and the
Fiedler children adored their "Uncle John." Arthur's encasement
was so tightly woven that even Cahill — a man who did countless favors for him — could not bring himself to ask a favor of
Arthur. Whenever he wanted Pops tickets for himself or friends
he came to me. He considered it a privilege to serve Arthur,
expecting nothing in return. A very large, exceptionally good-
humored man, Cahill smoothed over relationships on behalf of
Arthur diplomatically and helpfully.

On one birthday, Arthur returned to his dressing room after
the *Nutcracker*, away from the screaming commotion. He sat
down at his desk, Boston Ballet's birthday cake before him, and
waited impatiently for a knife with which to cut it. Cahill went
to look for a knife, found one, and, upon his return, brought a
string of autograph seekers with him. Arthur scrawled what he
normally wrote on each piece of paper presented, "Very cor-
dially, Arthur Fiedler."

"No more business, John!" he said.

"I'm not drumming up business," Cahill insisted, continuing
the line of little ballerinas. "A few more won't hurt, Arthur."

"Says you!" Arthur grumbled, as he autographed another scrap
of paper shoved under his nose. "That's it! No more! Take your
business . . ."

Every Sunday morning Cahill would pick Fiedler up at the
Hyslop Road mansion. Arthur referred to these visits as "walk-
a-little, talk-a-little sessions." They would walk a few steps, and
begin to argue. Arthur always took the opposite position on
whatever Cahill said.

Both Cahill and Arthur were healthy most of their lives, but on one occasion they were hospitalized at the same time, Cahill at the Deaconess Hospital for a hernia operation, Arthur across town at Tufts–New England Medical Center, with pneumonia. Bill Cosel, the TV producer of *Evening at Pops*, stayed with Arthur while another friend, David Mugar, tended to John. Cahill was back from surgery in the morning. When he awoke, his first words were, "How's Arthur?" When Arthur awoke that morning, his first words were "How's John?" Cosel and Mugar compared notes later that day and found that both men muttered their queries within a minute of each other!

In early 1976, Cahill's health began to deteriorate rapidly. I remember watching him take five minutes to cross Massachusetts Avenue from Symphony Hall, find his keys, and open his car door.

Arthur turned to me and said, "Isn't that tragic?"

Cahill died of cancer in August 1976. I have never known Arthur to be more moved by a death than by this one. The last time Cahill saw Arthur was on the most exciting day of Arthur's life: the Bicentennial concert on the Esplanade. They spoke on the telephone twice after that, but never saw each other again. A year later, Arthur was watching belly-dancers in the El Morocco Club in Worcester, Massachusetts, with three other long-time associates. As the women twisted about before the old men's eyes, Arthur murmured, "Cahill should be here now."

David Mugar, the friend mentioned above, is a Boston entrepreneur-businessman who did much to project the Fiedler image. A successful and public-spirited citizen, it was Mugar who organized and produced the Esplanade Bicentennial concert on July 4, 1976, and who hosted the annual December 17 birthday luncheon at the Ritz-Carlton Hotel, where a group of us would gather to toast Arthur. An ardent admirer of Arthur Fiedler, David has dedicated himself to memorializing him in all future Fourth of July Esplanade Concerts. Yet, with all his devotion to Arthur, David never asked for anything in return. "As much of a friend as Mister Fiedler could be, I never took anything for granted," says Mugar. "Because of this we had a fine relationship."

On another occasion, David said, "Arthur Fiedler was as well-known to Boston as Paul Revere's statue. He represented all the things that were good to the people, but he actually was a class redneck. It was very easy for the public to allow Mister Fiedler to conduct from the podium, but they made it virtually impossible for him to come down from his podium."

Mugar's father founded Star Markets, the supermarket chain with stores throughout New England. From time to time, Arthur would call on David for delicacies. He loved Dungeness crab, from Dungeness Bay on the West Coast. David, in San Francisco on business during June 1976, went to Kressie's, a famous seafood emporium, and had the restaurant prepare a dozen Dungeness crabs, which were then packed in dry ice. He picked up the package at noon, boarded an airplane, and was at Symphony Hall by ten that night. After nearly everyone else left, Mugar said, "Have I got something for you!" and handed the package to Arthur. Fiedler opened it and was stunned. Along with Ellen and several others, he and David drank Michelob beer, ate the crab, and did not leave Symphony Hall until after midnight. When the cleaning crew came in the next morning, they found shells all over the Green Room, and the odor lingered for several days.

*   *   *

Although in his early years Arthur took time out from the Pops to vacation or do nothing, as he grew older he became less and less inclined to relax away from his work. The European jaunts he used to take every summer while he was a player in the orchestra were distant memories. At the close of the regular Pops season there were the Esplanade concerts, then his season with the San Francisco Pops. By that time, the summer was gone. Touring began, and he was on the road over a hundred and fifty days each year. Besides, he was bored by vacations and shied away from them.

Arthur did have two idols — Arturo Toscanini and Pierre Monteux — both great conductors who enjoyed reputations for being honest musical interpreters. Arthur identified with them. He was highly honored to conduct Toscanini's NBC Orchestra, and after he was presented with a Toscanini gold medal of the maestro's likeness he wore it about his neck like a religious symbol all the rest of his life. Indeed, some people were sure it was a Catholic medallion, and that he had converted.

As for sports, Arthur never engaged in any and used to belittle those who did find pleasure in them. "A waste of time," was his reaction when it was suggested he take up golf. The only time he went to a baseball game was when he conducted a band in "The Star-Spangled Banner" before a Red Sox game at Fenway Park. He left after the second inning. He did enjoy an occasional boxing match either on television or in person. He was particularly fond of Rocky Marciano, the Brockton (Massachusetts)-born champion, who never lost a fight, and retired undefeated. When Marciano died in a plane crash, Arthur was saddened by the loss.

"Too bad," he said. "The world doesn't have enough winners."

Arthur's reading habits were simple. He read only biographies, mostly of composers, but also of those men he admired — people who had "made it." One of his greatest thrills was in meeting oil tycoon Jean Paul Getty, about whom he had read a great deal. Arthur often talked of his visit to Getty's London home, and how much he appreciated Getty's toughness . . . and his frugality, which was as legendary as his own.

"Imagine it," he once said to me. "The old bird has a pay telephone in his house for his guests. He knows the value of a dollar!"

During the thirties and forties, a frequent backstage guest at the Pops was then-popular Henri de Glane, a professional wrestler from France. De Glane was passionately fond of music. A tremendous hulk of a man, he became a friend of both Arthur and Chuchú Sanromá. He would sit backstage during a concert and weep while we played one of his favorite compositions. In spite of his rough exterior, he had the heart and mind of a child . . . and he loved Arthur Fiedler. One night when Sanromá was the soloist, De Glane stopped him on the way out to the stage, picked him up, and gave him a bear hug for good luck, almost breaking Sanromá's ribs!

After Michael Kalliher, former fire commissioner of Boston, became a trustee of the Boston Symphony Orchestra, he brought some new fans to the Pops — the Boston Red Sox baseball team. One night during intermission, Arthur and I introduced our first bass, Georges Moleux, to Walt Dropo, who played first base for the Red Sox. Dropo was powerfully built and towered over Moleux, a Frenchman who knew nothing about American baseball.

"Georges," I said, "meet Walt Dropo. He plays first base."

"What orchestra?" Moleux inquired.

"The Red Sox," Dropo replied.

"How many basses do you have?" Georges asked, shaking hands.

"Three," Walt stated.

"Must be a small orchestra," Moleux remarked, and left to go on stage.

Arthur's aloofness was, in part, like that of his father. Very European in manner, Arthur expected the adulation — needed the applause as surely as if it were the breath of life. But once out of the spotlight, the real Arthur Fiedler came forth. It was a hands-off, private allegiance to himself. He required no one, but he recognized that the spotlights would dim unless he cultivated and maintained a certain level of extroverted behavior to mask his natural shyness. Arthur was the true introvert who found it difficult to relate to others. The fact that he looked like everyone's mental image of the handsome, benign, classical conductor drew people toward him in spite of himself.

As Bill Cosel said, "Everybody who knew Mister Fiedler or called him a friend quickly discovered that they had a close and distant relationship with him at the same time."

Arthur encouraged members of the orchestra to appear as soloists — although some of his promises took a considerable amount of time to materialize. A master of procrastination, he could string people along until they gave up hope. In that way, Arthur was very much like Serge Koussevitzky, who once said, "I have the weakness to promise everybody everything, but I also have the strength not to keep the promise!" Arthur despised scheduling soloists far in advance simply because he frequently changed his mind. Often his secretary called a prospective guest at the very last moment, silently praying the musician would accept. Arthur never made these phone calls. His attitude toward soloists — as it was toward all members of the orchestra — was one of distant matter-of-factness. He expected no gratitude, and wanted no expression of thanks. He once told Cecelia Arzewski, one of our fine violinists whom he had invited to play a concerto with the orchestra: "You know, you don't have to like me to play with me!"

After Fredy Ostrovsky, another splendid violinist in the BSO, had played a concerto and had asked to play again, Arthur replied, "Okay, sure. But next time play something new." Fredy spent an entire year preparing the Bartok Violin Concerto, a piece never before performed at the Pops. The following season Fredy kept reminding Arthur that he was ready with the Bartok. Each day, Arthur kept putting him off.

"Why do you have to know the date?" Arthur demanded, glaring at the violinist, wishing to stare him down. "Are you going back to Bulgaria?" Fredy finally performed the Bartok with good success.

In 1938, after I had successfully auditioned for Serge Koussevitzky with Arthur as my piano accompanist, and had been accepted into the Boston Symphony Orchestra, Arthur invited me to play a concerto with the Pops. Of course, I was happy. It was an honor, a dream come true. The season opened. I had practiced diligently and waited for Arthur to remember his invitation. I worried and wondered, but hesitated mentioning it to him. Then I heard the stories. I went to him to pin down a performance date. "What's your hurry?" he asked, brushing aside my question. "You really don't have to perform if you don't want to." Oh, I wanted to — but I never did.

Arthur had no political affiliations. However, when Ellen registered as a Republican, he became a Democrat. He vehemently opposed the Vietnam War but during those years insisted on playing "Salute to the Armed Forces," a medley especially arranged by Richard Hayman.

"A number of people are calling you a warmonger for playing that piece," I once told him.

"So what?" he shrugged, ending the conversation before it actually began.

Although born of Jewish parents, Arthur was affiliated with neither a synagogue nor any other Jewish organization. Indeed, he looked upon all organized religions with cynicism. He married a strong-willed, deeply religious Catholic girl, but never exhibited the slightest inclination toward becoming a part of her faith. On the contrary, as Arthur grew older, he became more and more contemptuous of the church and kept himself as far removed from his children's religious activities as possible. Although they were raised in the Catholic faith, he avoided attending any of their Communions or Confirmations.

One Friday night, a group of priests visited Arthur after a performance. The usual spread of cold cuts, served to Arthur every night (and which he seldom ate), was on a tray in front of him.

"Have a sandwich, Father," Arthur offered.

"It's Friday, Arthur," the priest replied. "You know we can't eat meat on Fridays."

"Why not?"

"Because it's against our religion."

"Who made that law, anyway?"

"We like to believe God made it."

"You really think God knows anything about corned beef?"

"Arthur is a heretic," the priest said, turning to me, "but we love him anyway."

VII

On the Podium

THERE IS A BELIEF AMONG MUSICIANS that just as in nature every animal has its natural enemy, the natural enemy of the musician is the conductor. Arthur Fiedler was no exception. When he became conductor of the Pops, he bore a double burden. He had come from the ranks as a player and was now looked upon as a traitor, a kind of double agent — a colleague and a boss. From the beginning, Pops rehearsals were not as well-disciplined as were the regular BSO rehearsals. Arthur instinctively felt the latent hostility of the musicians, and it immediately put him on the defensive. Besides, having always been a practical joker during his years as a player in the orchestra, as a conductor he was always on the lookout for the same kind of behavior in the players. He knew that musicians rarely say a kind word about a conductor, and he did not expect it. On the other hand, he seldom, if ever, went out of his way to compliment a player. "I don't give a damn if they like me," he used to say, "as long as they do their job."

I have never known a conductor who enjoyed rehearsals more than Arthur did. His approach to the orchestra was basically that of an antagonist — a bullfighter in the ring, with the orchestra as his adversary. At the beginning of each rehearsal his cold objectivity would not allow him to say, "Good morning, gentlemen," or when women joined the orchestra, "Good morning, ladies and gentlemen." Arthur opened each rehearsal with a practically inaudible, "Good morning, Orchestra!" until at one rehearsal, Roger Shermont, one of our fine first violinists, answered, "Good morning, Conductor!" After that, Arthur merely said, "Good morning."

We professional musicians play with many different conductors. Some inspire us, some bore us, some instill fear, some turn us off. With Arthur, it was a combination of all of these. Conducting was a job to be done as well as possible, and he constantly reminded the musicians he expected us to perform the same way. He would often complain, "You are all professionals! Where's your pride?" And since musicians always react when their professional integrity is questioned, the result was that he usually got what he wanted. He could detect wrong notes or out-of-tune playing and never hesitated to correct these lapses. Not only at rehearsals but also at concerts, Arthur had an irritating habit of correcting out-of-tune notes in the woodwinds or brass by raising or lowering his large left thumb, all the while conducting with his right baton hand. Although the musicians deplored this, they grudgingly accepted the infallibility of his ear.

Once after discovering I had the reputation of imitating conductors, Arthur asked me to imitate him. "There's really nothing unusual about your conducting," I told him, "except that you end each piece with a kind of curlicue." Shortly thereafter, I noticed he stopped doing it.

In most orchestras, the conductor must remind the players not to talk while he is making some corrections or observations toward a certain section. At Pops rehearsals the deportment sometimes got out of hand, and Arthur would shout, "You're only wasting your own time!" Once, after a rehearsal that had been particularly noisy, I suggested to Arthur that rather than chide them for "wasting their own time" he cut the next rehearsal by ten or fifteen minutes. "Why should I?" he demanded. "They're getting paid for it!"

On some occasions, when things got out of hand and the orchestra paid little attention to Arthur's admonitions, he would leave the stage in a huff. He would return a few minutes later, say nothing, and continue the rehearsal, usually this time with a much quieter, more respectful orchestra. So at intermission one day the word was passed among the musicians that when he returned to the stage, no matter what Arthur said or did — actually, much of the lack of discipline was due to Arthur's own masterful art of provocation — the orchestra would be absolutely quiet. Arthur walked on stage to the podium amid a churchlike stillness. As he announced the piece to be rehearsed there was not a murmur. When he stopped to make a correction there was dead silence. As the rehearsal progressed, Arthur seemed more and more uneasy.

"What's the matter?" he suddenly blurted out. "Is someone sick?"

For the first time in his life, Arthur dismissed the orchestra five minutes early. As it turned out, he was not able to conduct that evening's concert, and there was a general feeling of guilt among the players that they had caused another heart attack.

If one thing was lacking in Arthur's musicianship, it was a sense of warmth. To him, warmth, emotion, and beauty were qualities that would come out if the music was played correctly — that is, just as the composer indicated on the written page. An eighth note was an eighth note; a quarter, a quarter. Nothing more, nothing less. He knew the instruments of the orchestra, how to balance them, when to bring out the principal themes and when to subdue the secondary ones. He had "perfect pitch," the ability to identify each note in the scale, or each group of notes, just by hearing them. One morning while we were sitting in his office there was an unusual amount of traffic outside. Someone was blasting his horn, and Arthur said, "that's a D-flat." "No, Arthur," I said, "it's a C." We went to the piano to check, and I hated to admit it, but he was right.

Occasionally, I would argue with Arthur about his conducting technique — which, incidentally, I admired. He had just rehearsed a Strauss waltz, and insisted on indicating every single beat in the three-quarter rhythm. The next day, I brought in the following piece and showed it to Arthur. It was part of a facetious trilogy on conducting techniques submitted by Ozawa, Fiedler, and me to the Boston Symphony newsletter. Each of us was asked to write a "treatise" on how to conduct different rhythms. My assignment on "3/4" time follows:

In order to conduct a piece of music in three — usually in 3/4, sometimes in 3/8, and occasionally even in 3/16 — a working knowledge of baseball can be helpful.

Imagine the triangle on a baseball field from the pitcher to the catcher to the first-baseman back to the pitcher. This is the basic three. Beat number one goes from the pitcher to the catcher, second beat over to first base, and beat number three back to the pitcher. Since a preparatory beat is absolutely essential (like a pitcher's wind-up), the conductor is well advised to start at the pitcher's box and take a firm swipe into the air toward second base before following toward home plate. This upbeat is one of the few occasions when the conductor has a solo, so I would advise him to make the most of it. He must bring his arm up with great authority and without hesitation and bring it down the same way, being careful not to commit a balk, for there is nothing more embarrassing than a conductor hung up in midair while the orchestra starts without him. If this happens, don't fight it. A good conductor must know how to follow the orchestra.

After you have mastered the art of the three-beat, try to forget it as quickly as possible, because most music written in triple rhythm is conducted in one. All waltzes are in three, and the best way to conduct a waltz is to give a good upbeat in the same rhythm as a full 3/4 bar, then get out of the way. What you beat after that does not really matter to the musicians, but the audience will expect you to swing and sway, so go ahead and indulge yourself. A few preparatory ballet lessons will show results at this time.

If you ever come across a slow movement of a symphony that is in three and has to be subdivided, you are in for a bit of trouble, but don't panic. Merely use the same baseball formula as above, but hesitate between bases. If this gives you too much trouble try to change the program.

After reading it, he turned to me and said, "Wise guy!"

Arthur's tempi were usually faster than most other conductors', which, he felt, helped sustain audience interest. With him, timing was the paramount consideration while preparing a program and during a concert. His time seldom, if ever, varied during a performance. Each selection he played by the Pops was clocked with a stopwatch, and the resulting figures were compared with the records of previous performances. As he grew older, his tempi did get slower. I remember a performance of the movement "Asa's Death" in Grieg's *Peer Gynt Suite* that kept getting so slow it almost stopped, but Arthur was completely unaware of it. He had a constantly running battle with the lower instruments of the orchestra — the cellos, basses, and trombones. "Come along!" was his admonishment. "Don't drag!" We knew he was really angry when he screamed, "Take off your overshoes!"

He considered the cellists his particular enemies. They were the cutups of the orchestra, the jokesters who played wrong just to irritate and provoke him. "Someone in the cellos is playing an octave too high," Arthur would shout. "Cowards! Why don't you own up?"

Of course, they never did. Arthur once told me he had been given the authority to fire anyone for insubordination. However, in all the years I knew him, he never once fired anyone, no matter how difficult the situation became. It seemed that regardless of what shenanigans took place at rehearsals, the concerts were always models of professional pride, and Arthur was very quick to forgive and forget.

There was an ambivalence about Arthur's behavior on the podium. At one instant he could be the severe taskmaster, and the next instant an old rascal, conducting "The Stars and Stripes Forever" upside down or beating it in three instead of two. This was a kind of inside joke that brought smiles to our faces and did not disturb the music in any way. Often after Arthur initiated mischief, he, himself, would become annoyed when it got out of hand. The times when Arthur and the orchestra were strictly business were during television broadcasts or recording sessions. Sometimes there were give-and-take conversations between Arthur and the musicians, even during a concert. On one particularly warm evening the air conditioning did not function. Our second bassoonist looked in Arthur's direction and whispered quite loudly, during some soft music, "It's too damn *hot* in here."

"Who do you think I am," Arthur growled, without missing a beat, "the janitor?"

Occasionally, Arthur's behavior on the podium became less than dignified. For many years, the Pops has been playing Saint-Saëns's *Carnival of the Animals,* a piece for two piano soloists and orchestra, a fun piece that sometimes turned into bedlam. In the movement "Tortoises," Arthur conducted like a swimming turtle, his hands waving in a breast stroke. Arthur placed a second clarinetist high up in back of the second balcony for "The Coo-Coo." When one reed tooted, the second would answer "Coo-coo, coo-coo" from its position. And Arthur would turn around in feigned surprise. In the movement called "Pianists," a breed apart, according to Saint-Saëns (he was a pianist himself), he composed it as if the pianists were bad beginners. When a wrong note was purposely struck, Arthur would leave the podium and pound the correct one until the lesson was learned. It became slightly ridiculous when Arthur produced a metronome from under the piano, then followed it like a teacher with a typical beginning student. In the movement called "The Kangaroo" Arthur jumped all over the podium. But it was in "The Elephant," a solo for the double basses, that bedlam prevailed. While Arthur leaned over the podium conducting as if his right arm were a trunk, Sanromá threw peanuts at the double basses. I doubt that Saint-Saëns meant for his witty piece to go that far!

If a string player practiced a particularly difficult passage in Arthur's presence, he would invariably cup his hands over his ears and grouse, "Don't expose yourself!" When asked about a substitute timpanist, Arthur smirked and said, "Every time he plays that thing, it sounds like he's playing on a wet mattress ... which he probably made himself!" One night before a concert, our first flutist, James Pappoutsakis, brought in a beautiful gold flute to show Arthur. It had been made by Verne Powell, a famous Boston flute maker, for Pappoutsakis's approval. During the concert after an extended flute solo, Arthur whispered loudly,

"Buy it." But then, in the very next piece, Manuel Valerio, our first clarinetist at that time, opened George Gershwin's *Rhapsody in Blue* with the famous clarinet cadenza, a low trill followed by a *squeezed* chromatic scale. Just before the orchestra came in, Arthur glanced at Valerio and bellowed, "Sell it."

"I joined the orchestra in forty-three," said Arthur Press, our timpanist. "I've always liked Arthur. For years everyone's had their run-ins or battles with him, but one thing I'll say about him, he never holds a grudge."

Fiedler could not stand for musicians having a few bars rest. In fact, he made sure that they did not rest. Arthur had Richard Hayman write into his arrangements parts for a fourth trumpet, or contrabassoon, or cymbals.

Some years ago, Arthur was particularly nasty to the first clarinetist at rehearsal. Patsy Cardillo, displaying his own fiery temper, uttered an epithet under his breath, and Arthur heard it. There was a moment of pregnant, ominous silence. Arthur walked off the stage. Later, Cardillo apologized, and became one of Arthur's closest companions. Up to the end of Arthur's life, Patsy Cardillo often chauffeured Arthur to and from Symphony Hall for concerts and rehearsals. Patsy enjoyed the glamour attached to escorting his famous friend — especially when they stopped at a traffic light and people recognized Arthur. One day while they were waiting for a light to change, a group of young-sters looked into the car, then at each other. Suddenly, one boy shouted excitedly, "Hey, look! There's Beethoven!"

Another time, Arthur accused Patsy of not watching him as he conducted. For the next session, Patsy lowered his music stand so that he could stare directly at Arthur throughout the entire rehearsal.

"What are you staring at?" Arthur bellowed.

"You told me to look at you . . ."

"Oh, stop it."

So, for the next session, Patsy lifted the stand straight up, hiding him completely from the conductor. Arthur took the joke. Later that day the two men were standing at opposite ends of the room, speaking with their respective cronies.

Arthur called across the room, "I can see your lips moving. Were you calling me an s.o.b.?"

"I wasn't then," retorted Patsy. "But I will now."

Arthur did have a running quarrel with the busboys whom he believed deliberately popped the champagne corks during the delicate pianissimo sections. He ordered no champagne to be served during any of the music, and no food, drink, or movement during the concertos that usually comprised the second section of a concert. The order did not apply to televised events with special guest artists, because the audiences at these shows tended to be fully absorbed by the music and not likely to order any food.

* * *

Although Arthur Fiedler's reputation was worldwide, he was the proverbial "prophet without honor" in his own country. Only on three occasions was he invited to conduct the full Boston Symphony. The first, in 1932, when both Serge Koussevitzky, then conductor of the BSO, and Richard Burgin, the concertmaster, were ill at the same time, and Fiedler was asked to step in. Unfortunately for Arthur, he received glowing reviews from the Boston music critics, thus virtually ensuring his never being asked again by Koussevitzky. On the program was Beethoven's Fifth Symphony, and Warren Story Smith wrote in the *Boston Post*: "It was a refreshing experience to hear the masterwork played straight, not whopped up or fussily interpreted. Arthur Fiedler conducted Beethoven as the composer wrote it, not as a Koussevitzky inspiration." We can only imagine Koussey's reaction, if indeed he read the review! Some years later, Koussevitzky relented, and Arthur was invited to conduct a pair of concerts. However, fate interfered. Arthur had accepted an engagement to conduct a small group of Boston Symphony musicians to accompany the then-popular idol of the teenage set, Frank Sinatra, in Symphony Hall. When Koussevitzky saw the posters in front of the Hall announcing the concert, he became furious. "Fiedler," he shouted on the telephone, "how you can do such a thing? How you can conduct the Boston Symphony after you perform with this Sinatra?" and he disengaged him. The concert never took place anyway; Sinatra came down with laryngitis and had to cancel. It was not until many years later, in 1955, when Arthur had already conducted the Pops for some twenty-five years, that he was again invited to conduct the Boston Symphony, this time by Koussevitzky's successor, Charles Munch. The reviews were again uniformly good.

Arthur once stated he was greatly concerned about the state of grand opera. It was dying a rather ignoble death, and he felt if it was to survive in the modern sense it would have to recognize the strong influence radio was exerting on the general public. However, he was positive that personal appearances would never be entirely replaced by mechanically reproduced music. He thought that radio or opera in the movies — he specifically called them "talkies," as we all did in those days — would serve to acquaint many people with types of music heretofore unfamiliar. He believed both devices — radio and talking motion pictures — undoubtedly would whet the appetite of many listeners to hear such music performed by real, live artists. "I think with the assistance of people of wealth," he once stated, "there are sufficient resources in this country to carry on opera permanently — all classical music, for that matter. Whereas the metropolitan and provincial operas, theaters, symphonies, and the like of European countries are backed by government subsidy, the classics in America should be assisted by persons of means, independent of official positions. In spite of the radio and talkies, there will always be a desire to hear music in the flesh."

When in 1960 Arthur was chosen Boston's Music Man of the Year by the Better Music Broadcasters Association, its president, Theodore Jones, of radio station WCRB, Boston, cited Arthur for his "significant contribution in the field of music, regardless of its gender and, specifically, for the better quality of music Fiedler has brought to the American way of life."

Arthur always took very seriously his podium function as a bridge between serious and light music. In his mind, there was never a borderline. He found classical listeners in our concert audiences enjoying the Pops and vice versa. He never voiced an objection to young people's listening to rock 'n' roll, but felt they would eventually go on to other music. Although he tired of it easily, Arthur was by no means unappreciative of rock music. As a matter of fact, he found most classical snobs more narrow-minded than youthful rock fans, who were at least willing to explore new areas of music appreciation. He was convinced that over the years there had been a great development of American musical taste. After all, practically every city in the country had its own symphony orchestra and was justly proud of it. Having conducted a majority of them, he was an authority on the subject.

His attitude toward his audiences was one of deep commitment, although he saw them not as individuals but as a collective mass. He was once asked if audiences inspired him, and he quickly answered, "Not at all. I'm just as happy making records, when there is no audience." The only occasions when he seemed to establish a personal rapport with the audience were during the sing-alongs. He would turn to them and say, "Please join us. If you don't know the words, make them up." Under his breath the rascal in him would add, "But keep them clean!"

*   *   *

Arthur really came alive during recording sessions. Here he was in his element. No audience to distract him, no special on-stage amusements, only the music to be put on tape as quickly and efficiently as possible. He never took for granted the fact that his records were among the highest selling in the world. Each new recording was, for him, the first, whether a Strauss waltz, a Tchaikovsky serenade, or a Beatles tune. Each demanded his — and our — meticulous care and attention. (In the back of his mind, to be sure, were the royalties that would eventually start rolling in.)

Each session was recorded in Symphony Hall, usually with the orchestra in the center of the floor. During sessions, the Pops would play a piece and then rest while Arthur would listen to the playbacks in the control room in the basement. He was an undeniable perfectionist. During recording sessions Arthur spent over half his time downstairs in the control booth listening to the tape, then returning to the podium to give instructions to the orchestra. Less percussion here, more woodwind there, build the violins, smooth out the brass, not so choppy. We would replay, and Arthur would go back to the control booth, score in hand. He would sit in the control room and conduct an imaginary orchestra while he listened to the tape. Back to the podium once more, talking on the telephone directly to the producer. More instructions. Sometimes he would flare angrily. Eventually, his black-rimmed glasses would slip to the end of his nose from perspiration. He would take them off, dropping them next to the score, and we would rehearse as he hummed, sang, whistled, and shouted, but always with his dignity intact.

The selection of music to be recorded was always a matter of discussion between Arthur and the recording company. Sometimes they agreed; sometimes they did not. But as time went on, the RCA Victor Company, then London Records, Polydor, and Midsong, relied more and more on Fiedler's uncanny sense of what the public would buy. One of the earliest Pops recordings, and among the most successful, was a piece called "Jalousie," a tango by an unknown Danish composer, Jacob Gade. Arthur had been rummaging in a second-hand music store, and came across a piano score of the piece, which he bought for fifteen cents. When it became a hit at the Pops concerts he suggested to Charles O'Connell, the RCA director of "Artists and Repertory," that it be recorded. O'Connell had never heard of it, and strenuously objected, but when Fiedler insisted, it was finally recorded at the end of a session when there were five minutes left. The piece took three minutes and forty-five seconds to record, and later became the first concert record to sell over a million copies. This took place in 1935; about twenty years later a man came to Symphony Hall and introduced himself to Arthur. "My name is Jacob Gade," he said. "I have just arrived from Denmark, and I want to thank you for making me rich." He brought with him a number of other scores, all of which Arthur looked at, but he found nothing to compare with "Jalousie."

In the early days of Pops recordings the BSO was not in the Musicians' Union, and to keep the orchestra from joining, the Boston Symphony bought its own record presses, which they mounted in the basement of Symphony Hall. Management attempted to make nationwide record distribution deals with small companies, invested a small fortune, and found it wouldn't work. In the meantime, James C. Patrillo, president of the American Federation of Musicians, warned RCA that if they recorded the Boston Symphony on the Victor label it would be boycotted by the union. Even though the BSO was the most prestigious symphony RCA had under contract, they did not want a court battle with Patrillo. The record company informed Symphony Hall that until the union matter was settled they would not further involve themselves with the Boston Symphony Orchestra. In addition, Koussevitzky found himself unable to conduct other orchestras, all of which were unionized.

Rather than fight what was obviously a losing battle, the Symphony Trustees reluctantly agreed and decided to reach an agreement with Patrillo's union. The fact that the AF of M union members included artists of the caliber of Rubinstein and Horowitz made not joining financially impractical. Without soloists, the Boston Symphony could not function very long.

In 1942 the BSO became unionized. Our salaries did not increase as a result of becoming AF of M members; however, we did receive a larger fee — nearly double as I remember it — for recording sessions with RCA.

Unlike conductors who conduct without a score, Arthur always had the music on the podium before him. When he was asked why, I heard Arthur grumble and reply, "There's the story about old Hans Knappertsbusch, an aristocratic German who conducted well into his nineties, and always with a score before him. Someone asked him, 'Professor, you've been conducting more than seventy years; why do you still use a score?' Knappertsbusch answered, 'Because I can read music.' "

(VIII)

"Evening at Pops"

BECAUSE NETWORK TELEVISION did so little in the area of classical or semiclassical music, the Pops seemed like a guaranteed success to Public Broadcasting Service and its Boston affiliate, WGBH. The first *Evening at Pops* program was aired in July 1969, five months before Arthur's seventy-fifth birthday. Two hundred and thirty PBS-affiliated stations carried the broadcasts, and the number has increased each year since its inception. Each summer series maintained a strict format — twelve hour-long programs taped during the Symphony Hall concerts of the previous spring season. Because the programs were able to achieve nationwide, then worldwide audience acceptance, Arthur's popularity became even more universal. The program, which entered millions of homes each week, won the prestigious George Foster Peabody Award and was nominated for two Emmys. "All the honors I've received," Arthur once said, "are to me nothing more than a pat on the back. But things have never gone to my head at all." He accepted the honors as part of his job.

Some years after *Evening at Pops* was first televised, when Seiji Ozawa became music director of the BSO, a musician was in a taxi on his way to a rehearsal at Symphony Hall. The talkative cab driver asked, "How's Arthur? And how's that Japanese assistant of his?"

When the Pops started its television series, Arthur came into contact with an entirely new breed of popular performers, some of whom he had never heard or heard of. No matter how famous they were, all were awed by the name of Arthur Fiedler; but to him, they were only guests who were there to perform. The famous names included those of Tony Bennett, Glen Campbell, Roberta Flack, Peggy Lee, Pearl Bailey, Dizzy Gillespie, Ella Fitzgerald, Ray Bolger, and many others. Arthur was anything but flexible in working with them. In matters of tempo, it was they who usually gave in. They were very respectful of the "maestro," and Arthur became used to the title and the deference. (We in the orchestra, however, never addressed him as "maestro.")

A rehearsal with Ray Bolger started the "Call-Me-Maestro" quote. Here is that transcript, thanks to Bill Cosel, our producer of *Evening at Pops*.

BOLGER: Mr. Fiedler, nice to see you, very nice to see you. Nice to work with you.

ARTHUR: Thank you, thank you very much.

[BOLGER *sings* "Put on a Happy Face," ARTHUR *is humming in the background.*]

BOLGER: Desist, please. I'm surprised, I'm amazed! This kind of music in these hallowed halls. Why it's desecrating these —

ARTHUR: Have to earn a living.

BOLGER: What did you say, Mr. Fiedler?

ARTHUR: Have to make a living.

BOLGER: He has to make a living at his age!

ARTHUR: Right. Please don't call me Mr. Fiedler.

BOLGER: I can't call you Arthur.

ARTHUR: Just call me Maestro.

The "Call Me Maestro" stuck, and it became the title of an Emmy-nominated television documentary about Arthur, filmed by Bill Cosel. It did not win the award, but it did take a year-long look through a magnifying glass at an American institution, Arthur Fiedler.

Arthur did not choose the guests for our television broadcasts. He was not familiar with television stars, and he felt one was no better or worse than the next. Although there were a number of television sets in Arthur's home, he once told me that television bored him. The guests for our Pops concerts were, for the most part, chosen by Cosel. He would discuss his preferences with Arthur and Tom Morris, the manager of the Boston Symphony Orchestra, then make his decision based on a number of factors: the current popularity of the artist, the sentiment an older name might invoke, and the overall appeal of the star with regard to all generations. Once Arthur suggested Elvis Presley. But Colonel Tom Parker, Presley's manager, demanded $25,000 for an appearance, so the idea perished.

One television season premiered with Bobby Short, the elegant Manhattan pianist, who played an "Evening of Cole Porter" — a performance he regularly offers at the Carlyle, a New York hotel on Park Avenue and Seventy-seventh Street. He played everything from "Night and Day" to "Begin the Beguine." The following weeks included Israeli pianist Ilana Vered, the New Seekers, saxophonist Boots Randolph, dancer Carmen de Lavallade, Robert Merrill, the Boston Ballet, organist Virgil Fox, Richard Tucker, Anna Moffo, guitarist Christopher Parkening, and an Old Timers' Night with ragtime-pianist-composer Eubie Blake, the ninety-five-year-old marvel. Blake always used to refer to Arthur as "young man."

One of Arthur's favorites was Pearl Bailey. Pearl had been a star for more years than most people can remember. She is a grand lady, married to drummer Louis Bellson, and, as a perfectionist, equaled Arthur. Before, during, and after a performance, Pearl played up to Arthur's shyness. She came late to rehearsal, complained that her feet were killing her, and took off her shoes. She thought he was a cute little man and told him he would make a terrific Horace Vander Gelder — the central male character in *Hello, Dolly*. It made no sense, of course. But it was great fun, and in the case of Pearl Bailey, Arthur seemed to shed his customary suspicion of flattery.

Danny Kaye was one of the first guest conductors of the Boston Symphony Orchestra who had star status in the entertainment field. A number of years ago, he walked into the tuning room backstage at Symphony Hall after a Friday afternoon concert. Since I knew he had conducted at a benefit concert in Philadelphia, I asked him when he would like to conduct us. "Any time you ask me," he replied. I took him up to the conductor's room, introduced him to Charles Munch, our conductor, and by the time Danny left he and the BSO management had concluded an agreement for him to conduct a pension fund concert in three weeks. As we walked out of Symphony Hall, Danny asked my name.

"Well, Harry," he said with a smile, "you've just gotten me into a big mess. I've never conducted more than ten minutes of music in my whole life!"

Danny was starring in his own show at the Colonial Theatre, and for the next three weeks, between performances, I gave him daily conducting lessons in his hotel suite. A record player was brought into the living room, and Danny went to work learning some symphonic repertoire. There was only one problem other than the fact that Danny had never conducted for more than ten minutes: He did not read music. Therefore, everything had to be done by rote. On the night of the concert, he conducted for over two hours and was an incredible success. However, he had difficulty remembering that a beginning beat is a downward motion of the arm, not the reverse. No matter how many times I told him, Danny could never get it straight. His BSO program included Tchaikovsky, Strauss, and Wagner — music on the "heavy side," as he boasted. But Danny Kaye is tremendously talented and has an infallible musical memory, and he doesn't read a note of music! He mounted the podium, raised his arm, turned to me, and stage-whispered, "Don't worry.

I remember. Down! We always begin down." Then after the Overture to Rossini's *La Gazza Ladra,* he looked up at the balcony toward Charles Munch, our conductor, and shouted: "Not bad, eh Chuck?"

Shortly thereafter, Munch cornered me. "What is this Chuck business?" he asked sternly.

"It's an affectionate name for Charles," I replied.

Later, Danny received an autographed photo that read: "To Danny from his friend, Chuck."

Munch knew we had become friends and often spoke about Danny's conducting ability, remembering the fact that after Kaye's first performance with the Boston Symphony, a *Christian Science Monitor* critic wrote, "By any musical standard whatsoever Danny Kaye is a great conductor." The late Dimitri Mitropoulos turned to me at Danny's first rehearsal with the New York Philharmonic and said, "You know, this isn't funny. This man *is* a great conductor!"

That night at a party after the concert, Mitropoulos soundly scolded Danny. "Imagine a man with your musical talent not reading music!" he said. "You must learn!" But Danny answered, "No, it might spoil me."

Jean Martinon, the French composer and conductor, told Danny, "You have a great advantage over us conductors. We spend a good deal of our lives with our heads in the score, then we try to get away from the score in order to make our music alive and spontaneous. You never had to go through that so you do everything naturally and spontaneously. And your music-making is therefore more alive and natural!" And conductor William Steinberg once stated, "All things considered, when it comes to conductors, Danny Kaye is still the best!"

Danny did one Pension Fund benefit concert with the Pops, in which he constantly imitated Arthur. It was one of the rare times when Arthur sat in the audience, convulsed with laughter.

Bob Hope's appearance with the Pops was not televised. Hope had come to Boston for his daughter's graduation from Wellesley College. He was asked by the Wellesley Pops Night Committee to make a personal appearance, and agreed. As Fiedler and Hope came on stage to tumultuous applause, two men carrying enormous cue cards stationed themselves on the floor in front of the stage. We in the orchestra were able to read precisely what Hope was going to say.

The most complicated TV show we ever did was *Sesame Street*. Arthur had to read a number of lines from giant cue cards: He was asked to respond to Big Bird. He did, but became confused as Big Bird kept changing his lines during rehearsal. He was called "Mr. Fuddler," "Mr. Foodler," and "Mr. Fiddler" — anything but his real name. The concert was a booming success. Big Bird danced with Arthur, and Arthur read all his cue cards perfectly.

Many people have appeared as guests with both the Symphony Hall Pops and the television version, *Evening at Pops*. We have had the more famous guests on the televised programs, like Roy Clark, country and western star, who, during a rehearsal exchanged his guitar for a violin and, midway through the piece, turned to the orchestra and shouted, "I got a lot of nerve playing fiddle out front of you guys!"

Jan Peerce, the great tenor of the Metropolitan Opera, said to Arthur during a sellout performance before the Histadrut (the Israeli Labor Organization), "Don't worry tonight, Arthur. We're strong. All our people are here!"

We even had nonmusical performers. Columnist William F. Buckley came to recite the Ogden Nash verses in the Saint-Saëns's *Carnival of the Animals,* and we all discovered a human side of Buckley that we hadn't seen before. When Julia Child came to recite "Tubby the Tuba," at the rehearsal Fiedler gave her an extended lesson in diction, pronunciation, and delivery. Mrs. Child took the instruction graciously.

Senator Edward Kennedy was invited to narrate Aaron Copland's *Lincoln Portrait*. His plane was late in arriving from Washington that morning, and there was no time to rehearse with the Pops Orchestra. Arthur, Senator Kennedy, and I adjourned to the Green Room for a hurried run-through. After the concert, his mother, Rose Kennedy, cornered me at a small reception and asked, "Did he rehearse?"

"No," I replied. "There wasn't time."

"I've told him time and again," she said angrily, "that he must take his commitments seriously!"

One Sunday afternoon in Pittsburgh, Pennsylvania, Frank Sinatra came to the concert. During intermission, he came backstage to be greeted by a number of the musicians. One of the people he met was Jean LeFranc, former first viola player with the BSO, a quiet, unassuming Frenchman who, although he had lived in the United States for a number of years, knew virtually nothing about this country or the people who inhabited it, and his English was entirely unintelligible. What occurred beyond Symphony Hall did not concern him. After the performance, LeFranc came to me, deeply puzzled, and asked, "Who is this man?"

"Haven't you heard of Frank Sinatra?"

"*Mais oui,* I know the Franck Sonata. Played it many times, but who is this man?"

*   *   *

"Arthur found it very difficult to conduct things that were not repertory," says Bill Cosel. Cosel quickly learned to be apprehensive about *Evening at Pops* shows that featured jazz musicians. "Rehearsals were painful for Arthur," Bill remembers. "Painful for the artists, who did not know what they had gotten themselves into, and painful for the musicians, who found these rehearsals laborious and full of nit-picking tedium."

After rehearsing with Sarah Vaughn, Arthur took a tape of the session home and tried to memorize every note as she sang it. At the concert, she improvised so freely Arthur was lost most of the time.

In the jazz field, in which neither Arthur nor I was overly familiar, few ever approach the stature of Dizzy Gillespie. One of the founders and ardent practitioners of bebop during the forties in New York clubs like Birdland and Jazz City, along Fifty-first Street, Dizzy plays trumpet with an ear tuned toward Gabriel. A large, heavy-set man with a small, graying goatee, Dizzy brought his horn to the Pops for another in our series of tributes to jazz. His appearance with the Pops caused some consternation. Arthur could not bring himself to accept anything that was not in his score, and before long, Dizzy was off on a tangent. Arthur stopped the orchestra.

"What are you doing?" he demanded of Gillespie.

"Maestro," Dizzy answered, "you just keep it a-going. Never mind what I'm doing." For the rest of the rehearsal Arthur attempted merely to beat time. But when the tempo began to lag, Gillespie turned to me and said, "Man, he don't know where *one* is."

I am not sure to this day whether or not Dizzy can read music. I asked his bass player, who was struggling with one of our special arrangements, "Do you read music?" and he answered, "Not enough for it to bother me."

A similar incident occurred with Ella Fitzgerald. It is said that Louis Armstrong invented scatting — mouthing musical notes without using words — but that Ella Fitzgerald perfected it into an art form greater than anyone had ever imagined it could be. A perfectionist herself, Ella ran head on into Arthur, and Symphony Hall shook. Her music was arranged for full orchestra, but not the way Arthur preferred it for the Boston Pops. It was too loose, not exact enough for him to conduct in the manner to which he was accustomed and the audience had grown to expect.

Ella required a quick run-through — if for no other reason than to familiarize herself with Arthur's way of conducting. She had performed with thousands of bands and orchestras during her nearly fifty-year career perhaps, but probably none like the Boston Pops. She began with the Chick Webb Band in the early thirties and, through the years, had worked with the best. But now there was the problem of her eyesight. Ella had recently undergone two cataract operations, and it would take some time for her sight to return to normal. She could barely see the podium. A stand was set up in front of her, with the music she would sing during her part of the program correctly arranged, but she sang from memory, never once referring to the music, which she could not have seen clearly, anyway. Wailing "S'Wonderful" was a listener's delight, and so was "How High the Moon." However, several minutes of the music were devoted to scatting. Arthur had no concept of what was happening. It was not part of the score, not written anywhere for his orderly mind to absorb. The audience, however, howled their approval. Even we long-hairs realized it was an artistic manifestation of jazz at its finest. Ella left the stage first, carrying a large bouquet of roses. They returned from the wings, shook hands, waved to the audience, shook hands again, and strolled backstage.

"Enjoyed it, Doctor," Ella was overheard to say.

Amid the hubbub of confusion accompanying the end of a concert performance, they shook hands once more, nodded curtly, and quickly parted — Ella to her dressing room, Arthur upstairs to his dressing room. The critics' reviews of the concert were laudatory. "Fiedler has done it again!" one wrote. "Boston is rapidly becoming the center of Jazz Americana. The Big Band Era, with the Pops at the forefront, is about to be reincarnated. Music is alive and well, thriving in one of the great orchestral institutions in the world . . ."

*   *   *

One of Arthur's most thrilling experiences with jazz involved a one-night fling with the classically trained Al Hirt on Dixieland's fabled Bourbon Street in New Orleans. Hirt is an enormous man — six feet one inch and he weighs over three hundred pounds — with a full beard that he grew for the 1956 New Orleans Mardi Gras carnival. His career bridged the gap between symphony and jazz until he decided to open his own club in the fabled French Quarter. It was in 1964 as it is today, a dazzling showplace, complete with showgirl-type waitresses dressed in scanty white-and-gold Grecian togas. Al had appeared a year earlier in Symphony Hall with Arthur and the Pops, so when he redecorated his nightclub after a busy summer tourist season, he invited Arthur to inaugurate the opening night. Arthur accepted. He had never conducted a jazz band before, and the idea of conducting a band of New Orleans musicians interested him.

"Arthur was returning a favor," Hirt explained. "The summer before I had guested with the Boston Pops. So here we were in my place having ourselves a jam session. It was out of sight. Arthur and six of my musicians. They had never had to sit tight for a classical baton before. My musicians were nervous as all hell. I know the feeling. I tried cooling them down, but no good. They had the jitters something fierce. Anyway, we got through a late afternoon rehearsal in good shape, and we were ready to go. Arthur was fantastic. We really dug him."

Arthur was excited about the performance — a new situation in which to perform. He enjoyed jazz, and felt people should be more flexible with their musical tastes. Some jazz fans shy away from classical music, and some classical music lovers — the snobs, as Arthur called them — won't listen to jazz. He believed both were wrong in their attitudes.

"It's all wrong," he was quoted as saying. "Look at reading habits. A lot of intellectuals also like a good detective story . . . a whodunit. Why can't the people who enjoy Ellery Queen appreciate Shakespeare? I believe they not only can, but do. The problem is, however, nobody wants to admit diverse musical tastes in front of their peers."

Al Hirt's nightclub was so jammed with spectators that two burly bouncers could not control the crowd. The police were called. They cordoned off the area with wooden barricades, and then they joined the folks there to listen. A thousand people greeted Arthur when he arrived.

"What a scene," Hirt remembered fondly. "The club was

packed tighter than sardines in a can. I could hardly get through the folks to the bandstand. We tuned up in a hurry. Arthur came out — people giving him a standing ovation — and we jammed. It was a gas. I've always strived to appeal to the masses — to the younger generation as well as the older folks. Arthur was the same way. He took pleasure in mixing jazz with the classics. Some of my fans became his, and some of Arthur's loyal following discovered me. It didn't hurt either of our record sales none, that's for sure. It was a beautiful night. Beautiful."

Ultimately, they recorded an album together. Arthur thought the original title, *Holiday for Brass,* was weak. Somebody suggested *Fiedler Gets Hirt.* Finally, Arthur came up with *Pops Goes the Trumpet,* its actual title. The album included the Haydn Concerto in D, "The Lost Chord," "Java," and "Bugler's Holiday." They were going to do another, but time passed and they never got around to it. Arthur was now very preoccupied with his new interest, television.

*   *   *

Martin Bookspan's piece for *Hi Fi/Stereo Review* in June 1960 captured some of the spirit inherent in the Pops:

I interviewed Arthur before the days of tape and the interview was to be recorded on an acetate disc for later re-broadcast. I asked Fiedler about the obvious good time he and the musicians have playing the Pops repertoire and he replied, "Yes, we do have fun, but we don't like to make it *too* obvious." During the broadcast, however, one of those incidents occurred which causes one to believe that the Fates do have a sense of humor. At the point where Fiedler was saying, "Yes, we do have fun," the pickup stylus ran into a repeating groove and played it over and over again until the engineer mercifully gave it a little nudge to help it on its way. But what the radio listeners heard was "Yes, we do have fun, we do have fun, we do have fun, we do have fun, we do have fun, we do have fun...but we don't like to make it *too* obvious!"

One example of conspicuous levity is to be found in Walter Piston's *The Incredible Flutist* (RCA Victor LM 2084). The work was an immediate hit with the Pops audiences, and Fiedler and the orchestra recorded it that season. One of the sections in the score is a circus parade, and at the rehearsals that preceded the premiere, some of the musicians began to "cut up" at this particular point, whistling and shouting. Piston, who attended the rehearsals, loved this extra bit of nonsense — even the barking of the dog, introduced by Boaz Piller, our contra-bassoonist, and asked the musicians to continue their merrymaking at the actual performances and in the recording.

Ethel Merman, whose personality was very much like Arthur's, came to rehearse with the Pops on one occasion for a televised concert. She was, musically, very professional. Her coldness and aloof manner never come through when she sings. With piano and drums, we rehearsed in the Green Room. Arthur conducted. From time to time, he shook his head. Finally, he whispered to me, "We won't need microphones tonight. She's blasting us out of the Green Room!"

* * *

At one time the orchestra reacted spontaneously to what could have been a very unpleasant situation. It was during a rehearsal with Chet Atkins, the country and western superstar. Chet is clearly a virtuoso musician. Unfortunately, he decided to bring a tape recorder to the rehearsal, which is expressly forbidden by our union contract. He was told he could not record the rehearsal. Chet said it was only for his own edification — something to listen to back in his hotel room before the concert. He also taped rehearsals as a method of improving his performance. We were sorry, our orchestra committee chairman, Bob Ripley, admonished, but no one was permitted to tape a rehearsal. Atkins got very angry. He told our man to shut up. More than half of the musicians rose to their feet in unison. Arthur quickly called an intermission, hoping tempers would cool down. Fifteen minutes later, Atkins was back, apologized, and finished the rehearsal, minus the tape recorder. That evening's performance was outstanding, and for us the incident lost its importance.

Oscar Peterson, the jazz pianist, taught us all something about eighty-eight keys and the ability to play them. After the concert, I asked him how he had mastered his instrument so completely. He smiled and said, "Played lots and lots of Czerny when I was a kid."

Robert Merrill and Richard Tucker, long established stars of the Metropolitan Opera, sometimes toured together during the Met's off-season. We were privileged to have them at the Pops doing several selections from *Fiddler on the Roof*. In the Green Room after the concert, Richard Tucker told us a story about himself and his brother-in-law, Jan Peerce. Richard and Jan were both very pious Jews. Neither would perform on the Sabbath. Once they found themselves in a small town outside Chicago on a Friday evening, sought out an Orthodox synagogue, and went to services. The cantor had laryngitis. The rabbi asked for a volunteer. Richard sang the service Friday night, Jan, Saturday morning. After it ended, the rabbi and the president of the congregation came up to both of them, and said, "We don't know who you are, or where you came from, but we took a vote. We'll hire either one of you for the High Holidays."

Roberta Flack was gracious enough to overlook Arthur's social illiteracy. Early one morning, Flack entered Arthur's office and, before she could announce herself, was summarily dismissed with a casual wave of his hand. When Roberta merely stood there, Arthur repeated himself, this time a bit more loudly.

"I do not do floors," Roberta replied, smiling. "I am Roberta Flack, Maestro, and I'll be performing with you this evening. I only do rehearsals, singing, occasionally write songs, and play piano."

"See that it's in tune," he replied, and walked out.

*   *   *

I was associated with Arthur for forty of the incredible fifty years he conducted the Boston Pops — his record, by the way, unmatched by any other conductor in musical history. Prior to that, amazingly enough, he did all the work himself, occasionally inviting one of his acquaintances like Charles O'Connell, the producer of our RCA Victor records, to conduct part of the concert. Charlie O'Connell was a frustrated would-be conductor who was vitally important to Arthur because of his position with RCA. I particularly remember a concert in which O'Connell conducted Glière's "Russian Sailor's Dance," and in his great excitement and nervousness conducted the entire piece beating up on the downbeat. He finished with his hands held high, one beat after the orchestra had stopped playing!

Each year, Symphony Hall has a four-day fund-raising event called the BSO–Pops Marathon, broadcast over both radio and television and geared toward helping us reduce our annual deficit. For any thousand-dollar donation, an amateur may realize a lifelong ambition and conduct "Stars and Stripes Forever" in Symphony Hall, with the full Boston Pops Orchestra. For over twenty-five years, Al Robison has been the Boston Symphony Orchestra/Pops stage manager. A giant of a man both physically and temperamentally, Al has always been another frustrated conductor. During his long association with the orchestra, Al had never heard the orchestra from out front. We musicians knew of his dream to conduct the Pops and we passed the hat among ourselves, raised the thousand dollars, and gave him his opportunity. It occurred on one of my conducting nights. I gave Al a few hurry-up lessons — none of which had the slightest effect.

On the night of his debut, before he came to the podium, I made the following announcement to the sold-out Symphony Hall audience:

"For over twenty-five years, our stage manager, Al Robison, has never heard our orchestra from the front, and tonight is his big chance. We can only hope the enormous success he will have tonight will not go to his head, because conductors we have plenty of — but where would we ever find another stage manager like Al Robison?"

Between laughter and applause, our assistant stage manager rolled out a white carpet from backstage to the podium. Al came on stage to a tumultuous welcome. He bowed deeply and, being the stage manager, adjusted the podium himself. Just as he was ready to give the downbeat he hesitated, then stepped off the podium to rearrange several music stands in the back of the second violin section to make certain they could all see him. He returned to the podium, looked at me in the wings and smiled, as though he remembered to always give the orchestra an upbeat. However, as the piece progressed, Al developed a tendency to follow the orchestra, which made "Stars and Stripes Forever" get slower and slower. The more it dragged, the louder Al would shout, "Come on, everybody!" Al was a great success, and when I returned to the podium for the next selection, I was booed, while several of the players made a mock attempt to pick up their instruments to go home. After the concert, Al was swamped with autograph seekers.

I do not remember any well-known conductors being invited to guest on the podium during Arthur's first twenty-five years at the Pops. There was, however, a young conductor, a Harvard graduate, who, after having won first prize in a musical quiz sponsored by the Boston *Post*, was invited to conduct Richard Wagner's *Meistersinger* Overture at an Esplanade Concert. He immediately impressed all of us, and later became rather famous in his own right. His name was Leonard Bernstein.

And finally, there was my own position in the Pops. At best, I would have to say it was a precarious one. Since 1955, I had been the assistant conductor, but still played in the orchestra when Arthur conducted. On the days I was not conducting my colleagues would look at me suspiciously and order me out of the musicians' tuning room:

"This room is not for conductors!"

I would wander over to Arthur's dressing room.

"You're not conducting tonight," he would say with a scowl, pointing toward the door. "What are you doing here?"

Once I made the mistake of asking him where I should go.

"To the men's room," he replied.

Once after a concert I had conducted, one of my fellow violinists took me aside and said, "That was a great concert. The strings never sounded so good." Before I had a chance to thank him, he continued, "No wonder. You weren't playing."

Another time after I had conducted the Pops our first bassoonist, Matt Ruggiero, asked me the following morning, "Where were you last night?"

"I was conducting," I replied.

"Conducting?" he grumbled. "It seems to me if you were well enough to conduct, you were well enough to play."

After writing my first book a number of years ago, Arthur called me aside after a concert at which he had conducted and asked, "Did you make any money out of that book of yours?"

"A little." I shrugged.

"Funny," he replied, on his way upstairs to the Green Room, "I never made a nickel on mine." (He was referring to Robin Moore's book, *Fiedler,* of which he of course had not written a word.)

"Reminds me of the conductor who found a shoe repair ticket that was more than twenty-five years old," I said, following him up the stairs.

"Start in the middle, Dickson," he replied, without looking at me.

"The maestro wondered if the man was still in business," I continued. "He walked down the street and, much to his amazement, found the shop open and still doing business. He went inside, asked the elderly shoe repairman if the shoes he had left were still there. 'The ticket's twenty-five years old,' the man said, shrugging. 'You should maybe wait a second, and I'll have a look.' Five minutes passed before the man returned. He looked at the conductor, nodded, and smiled. 'Be done next Tuesday — if you pay me today!' "

The Battle Between
the Sexes

Arthur Fiedler was an unabashed male chauvinist. In the summer of 1978, the refurbished Quincy Market at Faneuil Hall was reopened, and to celebrate the occasion Mayor Kevin White invited Arthur and the Pops to give a concert on the mall. (For years, few celebrations in Boston took place without Arthur Fiedler.) The players of the regular Pops were all in Tanglewood at the Boston Symphony Orchestra Berkshire Festival, so the Esplanade Orchestra was engaged. However, many of those musicians were also unavailable, so a number of substitutes, mostly women, were recruited.

The concert took place before an audience of thousands, among them Joan Mondale, the wife of the vice-president, who was a special guest of the mayor. After the concert we all went to Governor Dukakis's house where the First Lady, my daughter Kitty, served a late supper. As we were sitting around the table talking about the concert, Mrs. Mondale, an ardent champion of women's rights, turned to Arthur and said, "Mr. Fiedler, I was interested to see so many women in the orchestra."

"Yes," Arthur replied. "It looked like a cooking school, didn't it?"

Mrs. Mondale at first did not believe that Arthur was serious, but as the conversation went on she was shocked as she began to realize he was, so she dropped the subject, but not before she had gotten an earful from Arthur about the inferiority of women in general.

The next day I had to go into the hospital for my annual ulcer attack, and I received a charming note from Mrs. Mondale that read: "I certainly hope it was not Mr. Fiedler's and my discussion on ERA that gave you the ulcer attack."

Arthur and male chauvinism were meant for each other. "Women should be drafted as nurses when they become of age," he said once. His European manner and education made him a woman's delight and nightmare. He treated all women as though they were exactly the same.

When Arthur first joined the Boston Symphony Orchestra in 1915, the musicians were all men. During the 1955–56 season, Doriot Anthony Dwyer became the first female member of the BSO. A fine flutist, she had the further distinction of becoming the only female first player of any major symphony orchestra. As a first player in the BSO, Doriot does not play in the Pops. It was not until the midsixties that Carol Procter, an excellent cellist, became the first female member of the Pops.

Like all orchestras, the Boston Symphony hires its musicians through a rather lengthy audition process. An employment application is completed and carefully scrutinized. The player then auditions before a panel of musicians from the orchestra, who narrow the selection to four or five to play for the music director. Until Charles Munch, the person selected was always a man. Munch changed all that. When he became conductor, all applicants played behind a curtain. The women auditioning were advised by our personnel manager to remove their shoes so that the sound of their high heels would not reveal their gender. Consequently, the Boston Symphony Orchestra now has many women players.

Arthur's personal battle between the sexes became a matter of public interest only after the formation of the Brighton (Massachusetts) Pops in May 1962. "Nothing since women's suffrage has been more exciting for women!" exclaimed Mrs. Marion Sutcliffe, of Newton Highlands, Massachusetts, president of the newly formed Brighton Pops.

But Arthur burst their dream bubble of competing with the Boston Pops Orchestra's outdoors concerts. When he heard that the Brighton Pops, an all-women symphony of fifty-three members scheduled to play from June 26 to September 3, 1962, at the Metropolitan District Commission facility in Brighton, would overlap the three-week July Esplanade Concert series at the Hatch Memorial Shell, he told a telephoning reporter for the Boston *Globe*:

"I think it's silly to have concerts by an all-girl orchestra."

"We have no intention of interfering with the Esplanade Concerts," countered Mrs. Sutcliffe after hearing Arthur's pronouncement. "We can wait until the Esplanade Concerts are finished in the latter part of July before starting our season. Some of the members of the Brighton Pops are wives of the men of the Boston Symphony. They think the idea of the feminine Pops Orchestra, as a counterpart to the male Pops, a wonderful idea. They have come to an agreement with their wives that if there are two musicians in the family, it is all right for both to pursue their music. In fact, some of the men have teased us. They say they're going to don dresses and join us. It ought to be a marvelous experience for all concerned."

But Arthur noted that the Esplanade Concerts were free, while the women's group was planning to charge admission, and added, "I don't want to appear as the musical director of Boston, but I certainly think it's silly to have concerts by a bunch of women."

Even after being informed that Richard Hayman was a vice-president of the Brighton Pops, Arthur was unimpressed. When it was pointed out that Ellen's brother, John Bottomley, was secretary of the organization, he glared at the reporter and snapped, "Good sense has never been a Bottomley tradition!"

Marion Sutcliffe gave her Brighton concerts. For a while, the performances did very well; but finally, they were destined to fail. Arthur's opposition notwithstanding, there were other compelling reasons, not the least of which was a lack of money to pay the players. Also, the Women's Liberation Movement had begun to manifest its importance, resulting in more and more women coming into established orchestras throughout the country.

Arthur firmly believed in differences in salaries — a man should make substantially more for the same job being done by his female counterpart. He told one reporter that he was "delighted that the San Francisco Symphony has about twenty-five women players. It may help the orchestra's financial burden, the reason being that a woman can support herself on less than a man needs for a family." He was appalled to discover that women AF of M union members receive the same wages as the men. "It's a crime and shame that girls can't be content to powder their noses," he grumbled one day. "Before it's over they'll be demanding separate dressing rooms."

*   *   *

Ellen, to whom Arthur was married for thirty-seven years, was a model of patience and forbearance. She, like her children, adored her famous husband and, with her great good nature and marvelous sense of humor, was able to steer the family battleship through many troubled waters. Ellen was, of course, as close to him as anyone. But no one ever penetrated his stoic veneer. During his various illnesses when Ellen dutifully hovered over Arthur with loving care and attention, there was always the feeling he did not need her or anyone else. He could recover on his own. It was the Fiedler will power.

Ellen was, in reality, a loving, dutiful wife, whose entire life centered on her famous husband. Being Mrs. Arthur Fiedler was, for her, a goal she had attained, and she was fiercely proud of it. Ellen's disparagement of Arthur was her method of asserting her independence from his innate male chauvinism, and her lusty good nature tended to smooth out their divergent characters.

If Arthur himself was a paradox, his marriage to Ellen was even more paradoxical. She was devoutly religious; he was a nonbeliever. Ellen loved people; Arthur did not. She was outgoing and always ready with a warm smile; he was suspicious of everyone. For many years, Ellen's mother — the proper Bostonian — would not tolerate Arthur. Later, they not only accepted each other but became good friends, although he always addressed her as "Mrs. Bottomley."

"Everybody thinks I married a rich woman," Arthur used to say. "Actually, Ellen inherited just enough money to go to the hairdresser every two weeks."

"He would never have made the social register in Boston if he hadn't married me," Ellen countered, in her lilting, cultured New England accent.

*   *   *

He always appreciated a beautiful woman. Arthur was quite taken by the enchanting Peggy Lee when she arrived to perform with the Pops. It was late spring, a typically warm Boston day, and Peggy was recovering from recent abdominal surgery. To maintain a reasonably comfortable temperature in her dressing room, since this was her first public appearance after her operation, she brought with her a number of portable fans, which she placed around her dressing room. It was necessary for her to rest quite often throughout the rehearsal. After the rehearsal, Arthur remained on the stage at Symphony Hall talking to her. It was an odd sight: Peggy lying on the floor with her feet elevated on a stool, and Arthur sitting in a chair close by hanging on her every word. After the performance that evening, Arthur went to her dressing room and presented Peggy with a gift of a gold music box containing his picture. This was the only time I ever saw him give a gift to a guest performer.

Another of Arthur's favorites was Joan Kennedy, whom he fondly referred to as "Joansie." She never hesitated when requested to perform in a wide range of fund-raising activities for the Boston Symphony Orchestra. Arthur was instrumental in convincing Joan to continue her piano playing; she appeared, as did her husband, Senator Edward Kennedy, in performances as narrator in Britten's *Young Person's Guide to the Orchestra,* Copland's *Lincoln Portrait,* and Prokofiev's *Peter and the Wolf.*

Arthur was extremely proud of his two daughters, who grew into very pretty young women. His eldest daughter, Yummie, occasionally accompanied her father to recording sessions. During a scheduled break at one such session, while Arthur was listening to a playback, Patsy Cardillo entered the control booth and, winking at Yummie, chuckled softly, "You know, Arthur, if I were twenty years younger, I'd be calling you Dad."

"Yuchh!" Arthur shuddered, looking up at him in mock horror.

*   *   *

The other important women in Arthur's life were his secretaries. He loved to intimidate them, especially during their first six months on the job. "Never cry" was the advice each secretary passed on to the next. Arthur's last secretary, Emily Weingarth, was clearly his favorite.

"I liked Mr. Fiedler," she said recently. "I guess when I knew him he was getting more mellow."

Four months after she began working for Arthur, Emily was married. He gave her a large check as a wedding present, a most unusual gesture on his part. On the day before Christmas, 1976, Arthur presented Emily with a bottle of liquor and a kiss on the cheek, which was also totally out of character for him. Ellen came downstairs, saw the bottle, and exclaimed, "You mean his royal highness actually came across with a present? That's more than I've gotten in thirty-five years!"

Emily always drove Arthur to the airport when he left town

on one of his tours. She also gave instructions to his hosts as to his needs. She became acquainted with three quarters of the world's symphony managers through her telephone personality alone. "I had to be very authoritative on the phone," she says now. "I was supposed to instill the fear of God in them."

She also gave orders on her own. The flask was to be taken away from him after one drink, and he was to be allotted fifteen minutes for a press conference, and so on. Referring to Emily, Arthur said, "If the general says I have to do it, I guess I do."

When it came to women, Arthur was European at heart. This was often evident during his conversations with those who surrounded him. One such incident occurred when Arthur was informed of Bill Cosel's impending divorce. Bill explained to Arthur his feelings and the reasons for the dissolving of the marriage. After he had finished speaking, Arthur was thoughtfully quiet. He turned slowly toward Bill, shook his head, and said, "I just don't understand. She's very nice, and cooks quite well . . ."

(X)

"Fiedler on the Hoof"

No OTHER SYMPHONY CONDUCTOR IN MUSICAL HISTORY spent as much time on the road as did Arthur Fiedler. To a lesser man, his yearly schedule would be killing. Always going somewhere to do something as a youth, Arthur merely expanded the habit as he became older. He once gave sixty-five concerts in sixty-one cities over a ten-week period. The musicians for that particular Boston Pops Touring Orchestra were exhausted, but Arthur was exhilarated. At one time, he seemed to be crossing the International Date Line about once every three months. With the exception of May and June each year, Arthur spent most of the other ten months scooting from one country to another, conducting as many as two hundred orchestras in a single year.

In 1969, when Arthur was in his midseventies, he flew to Tokyo to conduct the Yomiuri Symphony, then returned to the United States with the orchestra to tour across America and Canada, winding up the forty-eight-city engagement in Honolulu. When he was asked how he could keep up such a strenuous pace, he seemed genuinely startled by the question.

"I'm collaborating on a book," he once told a Boston *Globe* reporter, in his modest second-floor Symphony Hall office. "I'm thinking of suggesting *Fiedler on the Hoof* as a prospective title. Seems rather apt, don't you agree?"

Arthur's office in Symphony Hall was rather ordinary, except for two eye-catching features. Behind Arthur's desk was a gigantic map of the United States. Brightly colored push-pins marked the spots in which he either had given concerts or had contracts to perform. Over his music cabinets were numerous fire helmets, each denoting the city that had made him an honorary fire chief.

Since no regular members of the Pops played with Arthur when he was on tour, he spent a considerable amount of time on the road alone and loved it. He always booked a single room with two double beds and took his office with him. Bills, scores, letters, contracts, paper clips, rubber bands, pens, and pencils with large erasers were always packed in a separate suitcase. He also took his own personal podium on tour. Arthur designed the guard rail surrounding it so he could not inadvertently back off the podium during the height of a concert and tumble into the audience. An electric fan was installed in a small opening he designed at the front of the podium.

After Arthur returned from an infrequent vacation to visit his old colleague Chuchú Sanromá during the midfifties, he took his Pops Touring Orchestra for another midwinter ten-thousand-mile jaunt of fifty-eight concerts, covering fifty-six cities in fifty-three days. In Troy, New York, the truck driver carrying all the orchestra members' clothing got lost, and they played in whatever they had been wearing during the afternoon rehearsal. In Cedar Rapids, Iowa, Arthur was accidentally locked out of his dressing room, so he conducted in a sweater. In Dallas, Texas, the laundry lost all his socks, and Arthur conducted barefoot in a pair of evening shoes. When asked why he never found this type of grueling schedule a chore — playing so often and, for the most part, the same music — Arthur was quick to answer, "It's not at all boring to play the same schedule. At each concert you have to get the feel of the audience, of the hall. You try, as in tennis, to improve your game each day. You have to keep up your standard of performance." He continued his assessment, "It's a new challenge. One thing I like about a tour is that you shed all responsibility except the job at hand, the quest for a comfortable bed, and the best food possible."

It was this quest for the perfect meal which, I suspect, was a contributing factor to Arthur's hectic schedule of sometimes over two hundred concerts a year. Granted, the music was important, but he was also a consummate gourmet — a man who loved to be in a fine restaurant's kitchen almost as much as he adored a good fire. Never able to resist the gadgetry in hardware stores, Arthur looked at the eating experience in precisely the same manner. Every city in which he played had an eatery that professed to have the world's best something-or-other. Not only did Arthur believe, but he sampled — and frequently. He would stand by the chef, orchestrating his meal with the same verve and zest he exhibited on the podium. He would dine, enjoying each mouthful of food as if it were his first after a year-long fast. Wine was always offered, compliments of the house. It never agreed with him, so he politely refused. He was known to autograph a picture from time to time as payment for a dinner. On tour, Arthur tried never to vary the schedule he enjoyed at home: small breakfast, major meal sometime during the early afternoon, nothing before a concert, and finally, plenty of food and drink after a performance. It was almost as satisfying a lifestyle as holding the baton — particularly if a bottle of Old Fitzgerald was handy to refill the hip flask he carried with him no matter where he journeyed. Regardless of what time he had gotten to bed the previous night, he was always in the car driving to the next city by eight the following morning — especially if he was in the United States.

He never refused an invitation to conduct an orchestra, no matter what kind. Some of the orchestras he conducted were community groups of schoolteachers, students, cab drivers, and odd-jobbers. These were fun, informal occasions.

Two things particularly disturbed Arthur on the road: heart-shaped watercress sandwiches after a concert, and conversations that began with "I'm sure you remember me; we met backstage at the Grand Theatre twenty-one years ago come this November!"

It was not unusual for Arthur to be invited into the kitchen of a Bible Belt home for a drink. Kansas City, Kansas, prohibited alcohol; however, Kansas City, Missouri, was right across the river. After one concert, Bill Shisler drove Arthur to Bretton's, a fashionable restaurant across the street from the Muehlbacher, one of the midwest's finest hotels. Inside at the bar, they ran into Isaac Stern, the virtuoso violinist, who had stopped for a drink and late supper after a performance at the civic auditorium. Together, they closed the restaurant and Bill had to drive them both home. (Shisler did all of Arthur's driving after Fiedler discovered John Cahill's habit of taking naps behind the wheel.)

Occasionally, Arthur left Shisler and traveled by airplane. On one such trip, returning from Chicago to Boston for a special Pops event in 1957, he found himself sitting next to Mike Todd, who was planning to give his wife, Elizabeth Taylor, the world's biggest birthday party at Madison Square Garden in New York. Would Arthur conduct the orchestra? The extravaganza would have approximately ten thousand "close friends" of the actress. Arthur accepted. On the day before the party, Arthur asked what arrangements had been made for the musicians and was dumbfounded to discover they had been forgotten, along with the music to be played. Arthur called Bill Shisler at Symphony Hall in Boston. A package of music was sent by automobile. The following morning, Arthur met with a hundred musicians in a rehearsal hall on Forty-fourth Street and, after a three-hour session, was marginally satisfied that they would at least play in tune. At the dress rehearsal the next day, Todd whistled the proceedings to a halt. In his haste to prepare everything, he had forgotten to discuss Arthur's fee. A hurried meeting took place beside the podium, the figure was agreed upon, and the rehearsal continued. After the party that night, the New York *Times* asked

Arthur what he thought of it. "That's one unbelievable night," he quipped. "It should have counted as at least a half-dozen concerts!"

In June of the following year, Arthur and the Pops drove to Portsmouth, New Hampshire, to appear in a motion picture, the Louis de Rochemont production of *Windjammer*. Moored off the Fort Constitution Pier was the Norwegian training ship *Christian Radich,* which was to be used as background for the picture. A cadet from the crew, eighteen-year-old Sven Erick Libeck, had played the Grieg Piano Concerto with us the night before in Boston and repeated parts of the performance for the movie. When the picture came out about a year later, the King of Norway invited Arthur to Oslo to attend the opening. However, it conflicted with a previous engagement Arthur had in Lowell, Massachusetts. He talked to me in the Symphony Hall coffee room. He had spoken to the people in Lowell and they were willing to let him off the hook if I agreed to conduct, but there would be no fee from the promoters in Lowell, and Arthur was to pay my fee.

"What shall I do?" asked Arthur.

"There's no problem, Arthur," I replied. "I'll do it for nothing."

"You will?" he asked incredulously. "But I hate to be in your debt."

"That's just what I want, Arthur."

Several days later, I conducted that concert in Lowell, Massachusetts. All went quite well, and I thought no more about it. Arthur came home and, as usual, was busy preparing for another concert. All the musicians got their checks for the Lowell performance except me. Rosario Mazzeo, our personnel manager and contractor for the Lowell concert, talked to Arthur, who happened to be in the office at the time the checks were being dispersed.

"You know," he said, "Harry lost money on that job."

"How so?" Arthur asked.

"Well," Mazzeo explained, "he didn't play in the orchestra,

so I didn't pay him. Arthur, how can you let Harry do that job for nothing?"

Grudgingly, he wrote me a check for $100, which is what I would have made had I played the violin that night.

Arthur toured the East with the Buffalo Philharmonic, the Midwest with the St. Louis Symphony, the South with the New Orleans Symphony, and the West with the San Francisco Symphony. In between American engagements, he always made time for Europe, Asia, and South America. During a 1971 European tour of the Boston Symphony Orchestra, he conducted a Pops concert in Bonn, with Joan Kennedy as narrator of Copland's *Lincoln Portrait*. Her husband, Senator Kennedy, flew in for the occasion. The next morning, Arthur had his picture taken in front of the bright green door of the house in which Beethoven was born.

With the Denmark Radio Orchestra in Copenhagen, he conducted "Jalousie," as an encore in honor of the Danish composer, Jacob Gade, who had just recently died and left all his royalties to the Royal Academy of Music. One reporter called Arthur the Palladin of Music.

There is no way of determining how many hundreds of thousands of miles he traveled each year; however, every major airline in the world afforded him VIP status. Arthur enjoyed waiting in the guest lounge, drink in hand, watching the airport traffic. He felt comradeship with the people working traffic control. Like firemen and policemen, they made life-and-death decisions practically on a minute-to-minute basis. He once spent several hours in an airport traffic control tower, learning the rudimentary facts about the arduous task confronting the men guiding equipment in and out of airports. Afterward, he told a reporter they were the "policemen of the sky."

Arthur's completely ingenuous tactlessness manifested itself with especially unfortunate results when he was on tour. He once told a Dublin, Ireland, reporter that the London Philharmonic was far more professional than the Radio Eireann Symphony Orchestra. In Detroit he was appalled to discover several of the puritanical leading citizens of the Motor City were vocally opposed to mixing music and liquor during a proposed series of Fiedler performances to be called Twilight Concerts. "I think," he concluded to a Detroit *Free Press* interviewer, "and almost everyone of reasonable intelligence seems to agree, that it is a very pleasant combination to sit comfortably, listen to music well played, and have a beer or a little wine, and a smoke."

Arthur once agreed to conduct the Seattle Symphony for two performances while their manager found a permanent conductor to replace Emanuel Rosenthal, who had been fired for perjuring himself when making application for entrance into the United States from Paris. Arthur was asked, "How do you feel about replacing Rosenthal?"

"He should have been more honest," Arthur replied.

*   *   *

Characteristic of the perpetual motion that for so many years marked his career were four months in 1972, beginning in January and ending with the opening of the Boston Pops season at the end of April. Arthur was then seventy-seven years of age. He toured Japan, returned to the United States to take the Boston Pops Touring Orchestra on a thirteen thousand–mile tour — including its first appearance at Carnegie Hall — after that, he gave two concerts with the Memphis Symphony and conducted eight more performances in a twelve-day period with the Syracuse Symphony. "Something is driving me," he told Stephen E. Rubin of the New York *Times* during a lengthy interview. "But I don't know what it is. I have that kind of nature. I just can't sit and twiddle my thumbs. I don't enjoy vacations, because I don't know what to do with myself. I don't want to lie on the beach and get sunburned. I've tried that . . . I don't know what I'd do if I retired. I'd probably just be hanging around waiting to go to the dentist, the doctor, or the undertaker."

Once when Arthur was conducting in Chicago he had a very

bad toothache. He phoned Irving Glickman, his dentist in Boston, and was informed that, fortuitously, Glickman was in Chicago at a dental convention. In fact, Glickman was staying at the same hotel as Arthur. Glickman left the convention hall for Arthur even though he was due to speak before the American Dental Association that day. He contacted a Chicago colleague, received permission to use the dentist's equipment, and, with Arthur, taxied to the Wacker Drive office. As usual, Arthur stepped out of the cab and immediately walked away.

"Oh no, you don't!" bellowed Glickman. "This is one time, dammit, that you're paying!" Arthur reluctantly reached into his pocket and paid.

Although he refused to give in to his illnesses, sometimes he had no choice. He contracted a wide range of maladies, each religiously reported, but he always quickly recovered and continued. No tour was ever cancelled because of a Fiedler ailment. However, there were a few close calls. One in particular was for the opening of the Macuto-Sheraton Hotel in Caracas, Venezuela. He complained of chest pains, refused hospitalization, and demanded a fresh supply of bourbon and nitroglycerin tablets. After conducting that evening, he returned to his room and was close to collapsing. A doctor and nurse were summoned. They remained with him most of the evening. By morning, Arthur proved, once more, to be a medical miracle. He felt well and was determined to fly back to Boston.

At the time, Ellen's mother was in the hospital, not expected to live. Arthur felt duty-bound to return home. She died soon after his return, and he took Ellen on a hurried week's tour to England. He was to conduct five concerts in seven days. As usual, he stayed in the Hotel DeVere in Kensington, a section of London in close proximity to Albert Hall, where he was conducting. Upon their return to Boston, a reporter asked Arthur how it went, and if Ellen enjoyed herself.

"Of course," he groused. "She accompanies me only on the expensive trips!"

These expensive trips, for the most part, included the ones Sheraton Hotels provided. The hotel company would often treat Arthur and Ellen to a vacation and photo-session at whatever hotel they were opening. One time in Lima, Peru, during an earthquake, the Fiedlers were in their room on the twenty-third floor. Arthur was shaving when the hotel began to rock. Ellen jumped into bed and began to cross herself. Arthur joined her. As Ellen recalls, "It was the only time he ever relied on my prayers."

Ellen traveled with him frequently, but not for extended periods of time — except Arthur's Far East tour in 1966, which lasted seven weeks. Usually, she would go out for a couple of performances, then return home to the three children. She felt her place was with them.

"Popie was always nervous in a new city or country," she once said. "It was as though he was making his professional debut." After the seven-week Asian tour, Ellen told an interviewer: "I've been married to Fiedler for twenty-four years, and now I've just been with him for seven straight weeks. You know something? He is tough to live with."

Center Stage

ALMOST EVERYTHING ARTHUR DID — especially in his later years — became an integral part of his legend. He never refused a photographer, an interviewer, an autograph, or a television sponsor. He once told me he would endorse anything as long as he was paid for it and it was in good taste. At one time, advertising Black & White Scotch whisky, he appeared in profile in many newspapers and magazines, holding a glass in his right hand. He was sent case after case of Scotch, which he never drank — he was a bourbon drinker — but locked the Scotch in his basement, where it remained until after his death. He was the only one who had the key.

For a while, he was even endorsing cemetery headstones and monuments. After some lugubrious music, Arthur would appear on the television screen, and with a sad countenance would intone:

"We all must die someday."

"I don't advertise for myself," he used to say. "It's for others."

The last product he publicly endorsed was Florida orange juice. When I asked him about Anita Bryant, he said, "I don't care about Anita Bryant. I don't even know her."

Arthur was anything but flamboyant in his conducting. It was workmanlike and unhistrionic . . . and not particularly graceful. Whatever publicity he did receive — and in his later life it was considerable — came to him without his ever trying to achieve it. Arthur certainly had a feeling — a kind of sixth sense — about publicity, but he never went after it. He was a born ham — in a dignified sort of way. He agreed to pose on the cover of record albums mounted on a horse, or surrounded by a group of beautiful women, or riding a burro down the narrow trail of the Grand Canyon, or dressed as a flamenco dancer, or strutting about in a white suit like an elderly John Travolta for the *Saturday Night Fiedler* album.

"Arthur Fiedler had a consummate knack for building the audience up to a pitch with a mix of music," offered Tom Morris, general manager of the BSO, "and sending them home happy but hungry for more." Michael Steinberg, former music critic for the Boston *Globe,* viewed Arthur's role as a showman with a much harsher eye:

The Boston Pops concerts aren't regarded seriously as a musical event. He is not a teacher of the masses. Arthur Fiedler and the Boston Pops are a slam-bang, cram operation for people who don't listen to music. Most of the stuff is what you get on Muzak. Arthur Fiedler had to buy his success at a price, and that price is dealing with music that isn't challenging. A certain defensiveness is part of his posture.

Perhaps Steinberg's observation of defensiveness is why Arthur steadfastly denied ever being a showman. He considered himself a conductor. Actually, he was a combination of both.

Irving Kolodin once wrote in the New York *Sun:*

Fiedler's feeling for period music is a long familiar fact resulting indeed in some of the most delightful records and concerts in this country today. The period does not matter so long as there is style inherent in the music; he is likely to seek it out and make it live again. We have rarely heard him do anything with the care, taste and incisiveness that he applied to his records — these minor masterpieces.

Arthur hated to speak in public, and I usually spoke whenever an announcement had to be made from the stage. One night in Providence, Rhode Island, he wanted me to announce an encore.

I said, "Ladies and gentlemen, Mr. Fiedler has asked me to announce this encore because I am the only one on this stage who speaks English."

After that he took it upon himself to do the announcing. After he announced the second encore that night, he looked at me. I shook my head.

"What's wrong?" he asked.

I replied, "Were you speaking English?"

Arthur once appeared as a guest on the *Tomorrow* show with Tom Snyder. Snyder admired Arthur, but the interview was a disaster. Arthur had none of his usual sarcasm. After it was over, Arthur asked David Mugar and Bill Cosel, "Well, what did you think?"

Mugar hesitated. "Pretty good, pretty good."

Arthur stopped walking and said, "No, it wasn't. I didn't have it tonight."

"Now that you mention it," muttered Mugar, glancing at Cosel with a wry smile, "it wasn't very good."

In the *Sixty Minutes* television interview about a year before Arthur's death, Morley Safer facetiously asked him if it was true that, like W. C. Fields, he hated children and dogs. Arthur looked at him squarely and answered, "I *like* dogs."

When Arthur was caught off guard, he was truly at his best. In 1966, he was made a vice-commodore of the Swan Boat Flotilla on the Boston Public Garden, a position that had remained vacant since Admiral Richard Byrd's long-ago trip to the Antarctic. He borrowed a yachtsman's cap, wore a natty brown tweed sport coat, and was petrified because he had never learned to swim. He had just completed a three-continent, eleven-day tour and had been notified by cable of the Swan Boat Flotilla presentation well in advance. Arthur made a little joke about being surprised by the honor. As a child, he had fallen through the ice on this pond and, afraid to go home, had spent the afternoon drying out in the reading room of the Boston Public Library. After Commodore Paul G. Paget made the presentation at the Swan dock, it remained for Arthur to assume his new office. He climbed into a seat while the boatman propelled the swan by a bicycle-pedal arrangement.

"Who's the guy?" a little boy passing by asked one of his friends as he pointed a finger in Arthur's direction.

"An old hippie," a reporter overheard the friend reply.

Back at the dock, Arthur was helped out of the boat. He doffed his cap for the photographers, and began taking fares.

Another time, Arthur was honored with the Sword of Loyola Award from Loyola University's Stritch School of Medicine in Chicago. In a brief speech, he said, "Some years ago a physician suffered a heart attack. While he was recovering he decided to study why so many orchestra conductors lived so long. He put a lot of records on a record player and tried conducting them in his living room, and he concluded that the exercise conducting gave to the upper part of the body is healthy.

"I drink as much as I want. Of course, sometimes you can go overboard. But at my doctor's advice, I take a drink before and even during a concert. Bourbon first, gin or beer afterwards. It doesn't do me any harm."

On December 17, 1969, Arthur turned seventy-five. Sirens rang and bells clanged all the way from his Chestnut Hill home to Symphony Hall as he went to rehearsal. It was a surprise birthday greeting from the Boston and Brookline fire departments. They were waiting for him on Hyslop Road. He opened the front door of his house and counted thirteen pieces of fire equipment. Arthur was genuinely surprised. "I kept sniffing the air for smoke," he said.

At Symphony Hall another and greater surprise awaited him: a 1937 pumper truck purchased by Ellen from the Marlboro (New Hampshire) Fire Department as a birthday present from her and the children.

"I've always wanted one," he murmured, mounting the cab. "It's a real beauty."

This present topped Arthur's monstrous all-day birthday celebration, which culminated that night at a huge party hosted by David Mugar. Several hundred people joined Arthur at a reception atop the Prudential Tower. I had been asked to say a few words about Arthur on his birthday and read this prepared bit of nonsense:

The celebration of the 75th birthday of a remarkable man calls for unusual tactics; and so we have engaged the services of a sooth-sayer, a prognosticator who has been able to supply us this evening with a clear look into the future. It is the year 2009, and the fol-lowing report was carried in newspapers throughout the world: "July 5, 2009. Last night Arthur Fiedler opened his eightieth season of Esplanade Concerts before an estimated crowd of one and a half million people. The concert was dedicated to the memory of his long-departed friend and assistant conductor, Harry Dickson, and messages were received from all parts of the world, including those from 150 presidents, 76 kings, and 45 queens of various countries. The most meaningful telegram came from the Tranquillity Base Symphony Orchestra, which was founded by Mr. Fiedler a few years ago, and with which he has given concerts throughout the Moon. The soloist for last night's concert in a concerto for the elec-tric guitar was the President of the United States, Peter Fiedler.

A good part of the audience was made up of the conductor's family, which included 27 grandchildren, 106 great-grandchildren, and 240 great-great-grandchildren, most of whom bore a strong fam-ily resemblance with their white hair and moustaches. After the con-cert Mr. Fiedler was presented with his 15,000th fireman's helmet from the chief of the Pakistan Fire Department. The helmet will be added to the collection in the Fiedler home, which has long since become the Fiedler Firemen's Museum. After the concert there was a party in Mr. Fiedler's honor at one of early Boston's old structures, the Prudential Building. Asked to what he attributed his success, Mr. Fiedler replied, "What success? There are still worlds, and planets, and stars to conquer!" And with that he left the party to embark upon his third trip to conduct the Mars Symphony Orchestra.

Arthur hated the fuss of birthdays. Once a delegation from the orchestra came into his office — it was the day before his birth-day — to complain about something. Before anyone had a chance to speak his piece, Arthur took the wind out of their sails. "I suppose you've all come in here to wish me a happy birthday." He winked.

The City of Boston decided to honor his eightieth birthday on the day before it actually occurred, and Arthur relaxed the situation by wryly noting to several interested reporters:

"At least the mayor had the good sense not to mention Beethoven first. You know, our birthdays are on the same day." (Arthur insisted throughout his life that Beethoven was born on December 17, not, as the history books had it, the 16th.)

John Cahill had taken him to City Hall on some pretense. He saw a twin five hundred–pound cake in the plaza and, not realizing it was for him, would have turned around to walk out if the flashbulbs had not started popping while the sixth grade choir from the Shaw Middle School sang "Happy Birthday." Then Arthur noticed Ellen standing next to Mayor White.

"What are you doing here?" he asked her.

"Eighty years," she told everyone, kissing Arthur's cheek, "is a long time in the life of anyone but Arthur."

He sliced the first piece of cake, then put the knife between his teeth pirate-style and growled at the photographers. Ellen saw a piece of frosting on the lapel of his gray suit. She brushed it off, as Arthur said, "Well, mayor, I see we already have a cleaning bill."

Arthur was presented with a framed copy of his Boston birth certificate and a Massachusetts proclamation:

Arthur Fiedler [it said] and the members of the Boston Pops Orchestra have contributed significantly to the enrichment of life in the commonwealth since the founding of the Esplanade Concerts in Boston in 1929.

And then the proclamation designated December 17 as Arthur Fiedler Day. That evening, thirty-five of us gathered in Anthony's Pier 4, a restaurant Arthur had frequented for many years. We drank extra dry martinis and ate smoked salmon and caviar.

We gave Arthur three "books" that night: *How to Save on Your Income Tax* by Skitch Henderson, who at the time was having considerable difficulty with the Internal Revenue Service;

How to Conduct an Orchestra or How I Made Arthur Fiedler by Harry Ellis Dickson; and finally, *Forget Portnoy — My Complaints* by Ellen Fiedler.

On the table was Ellen's serious birthday present. It was a metal sculpture by Bruce Friedl: a rakish-looking elephant trumpeting a couple of notes on a musical stand. The notes were *A* and *F*.

For days afterward, Arthur was in generally good spirits, which only added to that mischievous side of his nature that demanded to make puns on people's names. To timpanist Arthur Press, he commanded, "Artie, Impress me!" Percussionist Charlie Smith was, to him, the Blacksmith. After Charlie had played a number of *C*'s in octaves on the xylophone, Arthur shouted, "You make me C-sick!" He even named one of the music critics the "Back Bay Brahmsman." When Maurice J. Tobin, former mayor of Boston, came to visit, Arthur asked him if he was any relation to Beetobin.

He once told a reporter that his favorite cigarette was a Chesterfield because it matched his overcoat. One night, as we were putting away our instruments, we were rehashing the program, which had contained the syrupy Melody in F by Rubinstein. "Now I have found the antidote to the Malady in F," he quipped. "The Medication from *Thais*!" Arthur always used to call me Harry Alice Dickson. "Why do you have three names?" he once demanded. "Do I call myself 'Arthur Morris Fiedler'?"

Arthur's fame was bound to lead him to the unexpected and the controversial. For several weeks prior to his arrival in San Francisco in 1949, word had spread that Fiedler had somehow been connected to the then regarded infamous Tokyo Rose, at that time on trial for treason against the United States in a Market Street federal courthouse. An attorney acquaintance who had befriended Arthur arranged for him to attend a portion of the trial of Mrs. Ida Ikuko Toguri D'Aquino, the American-born woman who had made daily propaganda broadcasts from Japan to the United States troops during the Second World War.

Her sixty-five-minute show heard each evening across the war theater was a carefully selected blend of war news, music, and gossip. Tokyo Rose was sentenced to ten years in prison and fined ten thousand dollars. A portion of the evidence gathered to convict her was a tape recording, which heard her exclaim, "And now, boys, I'm really going to make you homesick with the Boston Pops and Arthur Fiedler."

Despite Arthur Fiedler's world-renown, it never occurred to him to engage a publicist. He was constantly besieged for interviews, which he never refused. Perhaps the most personal of all the Arthur Fiedler interviews was the one with David Hartman on the *Good Morning, America* show before Arthur's Golden Anniversary Pops concert at Symphony Hall. The ABC cameras came right into the Hyslop Road mansion. Arthur, Ellen, and Hartman were in the living room. Congratulations were in order, and Hartman offered them. Hartman asked Ellen about her thirty-seven years of marriage. She smiled, glanced at Arthur, and said it had been more like a hundred and thirty-seven years. Arthur guided Hartman into the library, settled himself into a wingback chair, and was handed a red fire helmet.

"It's a chief's helmet, you know," Arthur began, placing it on his head in a jaunty position. "Fire hats are distinctive, very attractive. In the old days, they used to be made out of layer upon layer of hard leather. Very heavy; sometimes uncomfortable. Now, they're made out of plastic, very durable. Good protection. Much better looking, I think."

The conversation drifted to Arthur's early days with the Pops, with the BSO, the Esplanade, and back again to his marriage.

"But what about Mrs. Fiedler?" asked Hartman. "Tell me more about her. Is she fun to be with? Do you spend a lot of time with her?"

"Yes, she's real pleasant." Arthur nodded. "She talks the same to a porter at a hotel as she would with the vice-president."

"And you had three children?" Hartman inquired.

"Yeah."

"I read that you don't like children."

"Well, I was quoted that way. Some children are terrible bores and terribly annoying."

"What constitutes a boring child?" Hartman pursued.

"Well, uh . . . a child who shows no interest. I think it's really my fault because our first child was born when I was about fifty-two or fifty-three and I had absolutely nothing in common with a child. I didn't know what a diaper was. I didn't know anything. I'd never lived with a child, you see, and you don't get on the same level with a child."

"Did you do better with them later?" Hartman wanted to know. "I mean, did you ever establish a rapport with them or — "

"Well, sure, when they went to college," Arthur smiled, "when they grow up, you can talk to them."

"Do you miss being a bachelor?" Hartman grinned, changing the subject.

"There are certain things that are better, certain things that have advantages. I mean you open the door and go out and you're gone. That's all. No questions asked where you go, who you go with, or what you do."

"Do you recommend that young people get married early?"

"No, I don't recommend that."

"Why?"

"Well, I think you meet an attractive girl and you're stuck with her. You have to try all kinds."

"You were forty-nine when you and Mrs. Fiedler were married," Hartman said.

"Forty-seven. I'm nineteen years her senior."

"For twenty years you were Boston's most eligible bachelor."

"Might have been longer."

"Did you meet Mrs. Fiedler when she was six?"

"Seven." Arthur corrected him, shifting in his chair.

"Your taste in women was always good."

"As good as what was available." Arthur smiled impishly.

(XII)

The Golden Anniversary

IN THE EARLY SPRING OF 1979, Arthur was approaching
another milestone, this time, his fiftieth season as conductor
of the Boston Pops — a goal never before achieved by any other
conductor in musical history. Frederick Stock, years before, had
completed some forty-three years as conductor of the Chicago
Symphony, and Eugene Ormandy was in his forty-fourth year
with the Philadelphia Orchestra, but no one had ever made it
to fifty. Arthur had vowed he would never retire, preferring to
"die with my boots on," as he was so fond of saying. Considering his recent serious illness, the question around Symphony Hall
was, "Will he make it?"

Arthur's last birthday, his eighty-fourth, in December 1978,
had been celebrated in a hospital room on the fifth floor of the
Tufts–New England Medical Center, where he had undergone
surgery to remove fluid from his brain the previous Monday
night. The hospital listed his condition as stable; Arthur felt he
was improving daily. Dr. R. Michael Scott, who performed the
surgery that week, had given permission for a birthday party.
Ellen and Peter had hastily gotten the party together. Tom
Morris and Gideon Toeplitz were there, representing the Symphony Hall management; David Mugar; Bill Shisler; Bill Cosel;

Anthony Athanas, Peter Holt, and chef Raymond Buch, from Athanas's Pier 4 Restaurant; Johanna (Yummie) and Debbie telephoned birthday greetings from New York.

Arthur was sitting up in bed, wearing a brightly colored Japanese kimono. Chef Buch served him a birthday meal of fish chowder, caviar, and fresh strawberries, which he barely tasted. It was presented on a table that Athanas wheeled in from the hall. In the center was a bouquet of red roses.

Athanas gave Arthur a rare bottle of New York estate wine for a New Year's present and a supply of cheesecake for the nurses' station beyond Arthur's room. The party lasted a little more than twenty minutes.

"It was the best medication Arthur could have," Ellen said afterward. "It bucked up his spirits."

We sang "Happy Birthday." I conducted while Arthur was trying to project himself out of bed. When he could not, he covered both ears, and shouted, "You're out of tune!"

We left him in the midst of a huge pile of birthday cards, Christmas greetings, and get-well notes. The vast majority of the mail was from people Arthur did not know, would never meet.

Never very sure on his feet when he grew older, I wondered what the Fiedler Shuffle would be like — if he ever left the hospital. It was hard to accept the fact that "the debutante's delight and mother's despair" was now nothing more than a shell. However, he walked out of the hospital on his own less than two weeks later, more physically fit than I had seen him in recent years, though his heart had weakened to a point where his doctors could only marvel at his tenacity.

Arthur recovered, but he was not quite the same man. The vigor and desire to live seemed only a fond memory; however, the necessity to conduct, to return to the podium, was as strong as ever. The thought of not working was abhorrent to him. He was desperate to be back in charge of "Fiedler's Concentration Camp," as the musicians used to call the Pops. Soon after he left the hospital, a recording session was scheduled to take place.

Tom Morris alerted me to be ready to conduct a new album, *Saturday Night Fiedler*. On the day of the session, I came to Symphony Hall early and received a telephone call from Arthur.

"Harry, I'm all dressed, and I'm coming in."

"Okay, Arthur," I said.

But a few minutes later I received a call from Tom Morris, who had just arrived at Arthur's home.

"Harry," he whispered to me, "he's in no condition to leave the house, much less conduct."

Morris told me later that it took a great deal of persuasion on his and Ellen's part to get Arthur back into bed. The recording session took place on schedule, and we finished one side of the album that morning.

Two days later, when the second session was scheduled — this one to be called "Bach-o-Mania" — the same telephone drama was repeated. Arthur again called me at Symphony Hall in the morning to say that he was coming in. Tom Morris again called me immediately afterward. Arthur was still in no condition to conduct. It is ironic that the very last Fiedler album, with the picture of him on the cover strutting dance steps in a white suit, should have been conducted by me. When the album was released, a statement appeared on the jacket under Arthur's signature thanking me and all concerned. It did not definitely state that I conducted. Subsequently, our management informed Midsong Records that they were to correct the misimpression. They did so by attaching a pressure-sensitive label to the cellophane wrap on the jacket, indicating that Harry Ellis Dickson conducted the album; however, when I removed the cellophane from my copy, "Harry Ellis Dickson" disappeared.

By now, Yummie was working in the public relations department of the Metropolitan Opera; Deborah was married and a successful lawyer in New York; and Peter, though still involved with a rock band, was now in television production. The fact that Arthur would be the last Fiedler in the Boston Symphony Orchestra did not bother him.

"Who cares?" he once remarked to Ellen and me after returning home from an extensive tour. "Why should I? Yummie, Debbie, and Peter want to do things their own way. I won't be here, so what the hell does it matter?"

And it did not. Once known to party till dawn, to go where the spirit moved him, he now seemed devoid of energy — the sparkle and drive that had been so long a part of the Fiedler legend were gone. He was content to repair to the library, surrounded by his memorabilia — the honorary degrees from Tufts and Harvard, the plaques commemorating his membership as a chevalier in the French Legion of Honor, the scroll making him a Kentucky Colonel, the large collection of miniature musical scores, the few scale models of the New Bedford, Massachusetts, whaling ships, and his books.

*   *   *

Arthur arose on the morning of May 1, 1979, a little later than usual. Since the surgery, he was doing everything a little more slowly, with a somewhat greater effort. He came downstairs from his quarters dressed in his ragged bathrobe. He and Ellen sat at the kitchen table. After breakfast, Ellen told him, "You know what I want you to do now?"

"Don't remind me," he grumbled.

"I want you to go right back to bed," she said firmly.

He returned to his room, and studied the scores of the music he was going to conduct that night at Symphony Hall.

*   *   *

In the winter of 1979, as he was approaching this anniversary concert, he had decided to ask some well-known composers to write something auspicious for the occasion, among them Robert Russell Bennett and Morton Gould. Arthur asked his secretary to call Mr. Bennett in New York and after a short conversation was assured that Mr. Bennett would write a march.

A few weeks went by and Arthur, knowing how quickly Robert Russell Bennett worked, began to wonder why he had not heard from him. He asked our librarian, Victor Alpert, to call Bennett again.

"Mr. Bennett, this is Victor Alpert of the Boston Pops. We were wondering how soon we could expect the march," Alpert inquired, sidestepping the question.

"What march?" Bennett asked curiously.

"The one Mr. Fiedler called you about several weeks ago — "

"I know nothing about a march — I've never spoken to Arthur Fiedler," said Bennett. "Besides," he continued. "I'm afraid I can't do anything about it now, anyway. I'm on my way to Europe."

When Arthur was told about this he was puzzled.

"Who did I talk to?" he asked Emily Weingarth, his secretary.

She made a quick check of her personal telephone directory, only to discover that her number for Robert Russell Bennett differed from the library's number. Victor Alpert then called the original telephone in New York.

"Did Arthur Fiedler telephone you some weeks ago?" Alpert inquired.

"Someone did call me," the man admitted finally. "He said he was Arthur Fiedler, but I thought it was a practical joke.

"I guess my telephone number used to belong to Robert Russell Bennett."

"But that really was Mr. Fiedler," insisted Alpert.

"Hey, wait!" the other man shouted. "I'm an actor and I've dabbled in music myself. If you want a march, I'll be glad to write one for — "

"No, thank you." Alpert sighed, and hung up.

Morton Gould did write a piece for the occasion. It was a march called "Cheers!" and he wrote it as a "tribute to Fiedler and the Orchestra. He started to conduct my music when I was very young, maybe forty years ago or more." The march was dedicated to Arthur and its theme was based chiefly on the two notes *A* and *F* for Arthur's initials.

*   *   *

The day before the momentous occasion, Arthur had rehearsed the orchestra in Gould's march. He had not conducted that rehearsal with his usual crispness. During the intermission, he shuffled off stage to his dressing room. Al Robison, the stage manager, offered him a cold beer. He refused. He settled for coffee — quite a departure from the way it used to be in the old days.

He went through the Gould composition one final time and went home. With the exception of the Gould march — a jaunty ceremonial work — the program was vintage Fiedler that included Shostakovich, Offenbach's Overture to *La Belle Hélène*, Lehar's "Gold and Silver Waltzes," George Gershwin's *An American in Paris, Hair*, bits of the *Saturday Night Fiedler* album, and of course, "Stars and Stripes Forever." In the middle section, we would do Gershwin's *Rhapsody in Blue*, with Earl Wild playing the piano solo. Wild had been a favorite of Arthur's for over a quarter of a century, and their recording together of the Gershwin Rhapsody had been a crucial steppingstone in Wild's career.

"I remembered the day I met him," Wild said at intermission. "He looked at me and said, 'Do you play in time?' I was startled, but replied, 'I think so.' We've been friends ever since."

At 7:30 P.M., Arthur arrived. He appeared to be weaker than I had ever remembered seeing him, a little less jaunty than Morton Gould must have envisioned when he wrote his new march, but just as feisty as ever. He was taken up to the Green Room by the Symphony Hall freight elevator while he complained, "I can walk!"

A stack of telegrams and messages lay on the Green Room table. The Symphony Hall switchboard was flooded with calls. Reporters and photographers crowded about him. Arthur seemed oblivious of their presence. The telegrams were casually mentioned again.

"I'll read them later," he said.

"Are you nervous?" someone asked him.

"Sure, I'm nervous," he grunted. "Just as I was fifty years ago. I guess you have a right to get nervous once every fifty years."

"This is the opening of the Pops' ninety-fourth season," a reporter reminded him.

"And I've been around for all but ten of them," Arthur quipped.

The children came into the Green Room. They kissed their mother, nodded to their father, and were escorted to the Hall.

A few of the congratulatory messages were read:

Leonard Bernstein: "I continually thank God for Arthur Fiedler, at whose hands I first heard live orchestral music."

Ray Bolger: "My appearance with you at the Pops was the most successful evening I ever had in my whole life."

George Shearing: "You have done more to popularize classical music than anyone I know."

Benny Goodman: "I'm glad to have you back 'in the swing' again."

Roberta Peters: "Congratulations on your incredible Fiftieth Anniversary. The next time I sing with you please don't rap my knuckles with your baton for stealing an extra bow."

Roy Clark: "I just hope that maybe somewhere along the line, I can bring as much happiness and joy to as many people as you have with your music."

Anna Moffo: "Over the years how very much you have given to so very many. I feel very privileged to have been able to work with you."

André Kostelanetz: "It is impossible to evaluate the happiness and pleasure you have given to so many through more than half a century."

Chet Atkins: "The highest point of my career was appearing with you in concerts and on records."

Itzhak Perlman: "Mazel *tov* on your wonderful recovery. I remember with great pleasure our last concert together with the Boston Pops and hope to have the opportunity to do it again many times in the future."

Jesús-Maria Sanromá: "Ave Fiedler! Palman qui meruit ferat! Applause for those who are worthy of it!"

Isaac Stern: "To Fiedler from the fiddler — may the second fifty be as brilliant, as warming, and as cherished by music lovers as the first."

Senator Edward Kennedy: "Arthur Fiedler personifies the spirit of Boston. His music has been the constant uplifting force throughout fifty of the most exciting years in American history."

There were more. Hundreds of them. From every corner of the globe people remembered — the same as people in the Green Room recalled what they considered to be classic Fiedlerisms:

"I do not try to be loved — I just try to make good music!"

Concerning money: "I've never actively tried to acquire it. But when I get it, I hold on to it. Why not? I've earned it."

The Green Room was cleared. Ellen kissed Arthur and squeezed his shoulder reassuringly. I adjusted his suspenders. Cecile Gervais, the Fiedlers' longtime housekeeper, inspected his appearance one last time.

At 8:00 P.M., WGBH-TV began its live nationwide telecast. Moments later, Arthur shuffled to the podium. The entire audience were on their feet. Arthur took his usual matter-of-fact bow, then turned to the orchestra for the opening piece on the program — Morton Gould's "Cheers!" Then came the Offenbach, Shostakovich, Lehar, and *An American in Paris*. Arthur's conducting that night displayed no hint of what he might have felt, but the first section ended to another standing ovation.

Arthur returned to his dressing room at the intermission. In the second part, Earl Wild played *Rhapsody in Blue*. Backstage after his performance, he told a group of reporters: "It all went well tonight, I thought, and the maestro caught everything. What an iron will this man has!"

In the closing portion of the program, we played a rousing medley from *Hair* and selections from the *Saturday Night Fiedler* album. And then at the end, Arthur's signature, "Stars and Stripes Forever." The piccolos stood. The American flag unfurled in the background, and the brasses rose, and a cascade of balloons descended from the ceiling.

Arthur looked exhausted when he returned to the Green Room, and for the first time in his life after a performance, he went meekly home with Ellen.

"He said he was tired," reported Boston Symphony Orchestra manager Tom Morris. "But he is also pleased with himself. He has a right to be — he has just opened his fiftieth season and not many people get the chance to do that. Now he deserves a good night's rest."

Even the critics were moved by the concert. "*An American in Paris*," noted the Boston *Globe*, "was better than the one delivered to the populace of Peking, China, by the Boston Symphony Orchestra a few weeks ago."

"His selections last night," commented the New York *Times*, "represented his traditional programming blend of light classical and popular music that for generations has sent audiences away flushed with the feeling of having had a cultural experience and fun at the same time. Last night's performance was a most enjoyable occasion."

After this Golden Anniversary concert, I saw Arthur a few times — but only once again on the podium.

On Saturday evening, May 5, Arthur conducted his last concert. The soloist was James Galway, famous Irish flutist. After his last bow, Arthur returned to the Green Room and collapsed in his armchair. The paramedics were called. Cleve Morrison, our assistant stage manager, came to the tuning room looking for me. "Arthur has been asking for you," he said. I was surprised and somewhat flattered. As I walked through the Green Room door, Arthur was being gently lifted onto a gurney. Ellen was on his right, holding his hand tightly in her own. An oxygen mask was across Arthur's face. He was sickly gray. His sunken eyes seemed to have disappeared into his head.

"Here I am, Arthur," I said.

Pushing away the oxygen mask with his left hand, he slowly

turned his head and, flicking the tip of his tongue across his dry lips, whispered, "Did you steal my baton?"

"No, Arthur," I replied. "Not this time. It's right there on your desk."

He smiled sardonically and closed his eyes as he was wheeled out.

I picked up the fifty-cent baton imprinted with his signature and looked at it sadly, shaking my head. That was Arthur — a combination of conductor and rascal — a man trying to appear more concerned about a fifty-cent baton than his own health.

*   *   *

In April 1979, when Arthur had begun to fail, Tom Morris sent fourteen of us a memorandum marked "Very Sensitive and Confidential." It described step by step all the procedures to be followed in case Arthur was taken ill on the podium. All the announcements that would be made in such an emergency were already written, including the announcement that I would conduct the remainder of the program. Bach's "Air on the G String" was selected to close the concert, performed without a conductor, in the event that Arthur died while the concert was still in progress. Morris ended the three-page message by adding:

"I am sorry for the somewhat ghoulish nature of this memorandum, but we should be well prepared for these eventualities. If something happens, everything will be very chaotic, and it is our responsibility to act coolly and clearly."

In the meantime, despite his advancing age, Arthur was constantly busy with his own paperwork. He referred to contracts as "dog tags," and he rarely signed one until after he had conducted the concert. He did become forgetful, however, and drove the BSO treasurer to distraction by losing paychecks and claiming he was never paid.

During the last weeks of his life Arthur was constantly in Ellen's company. She hardly ever left him alone. Emily Weingarth would come over during the day when Ellen was busy with chores outside the house and get him to do paperwork, as a way of occupying his time. Emily told me she would never forget the day she was collecting her things to leave while Arthur was dozing and Ellen was standing by the foot of his bed. Arthur gently opened his eyes, smiled weakly, and said,

"I hope you didn't mind baby-sitting me today."

Arthur's bedroom had a huge African rug on the wall behind his bed. His bedspread bore a giant circle in the center with the initials *AF* embroidered within. Off to the side rested his short-wave radio. He could reach places all over America on it; he used it late at night during his bouts with insomnia.

*   *   *

The night before the July 4, 1979, Esplanade Concert was a moving experience for me. The next day would be the first time Arthur would not conduct on Independence Day since 1929. Ellen and I sat in the bedroom with Arthur for a long time in deep silence. I told him frankly that I was a little uncomfortable about conducting the next day. I could feel the pleasure he received when I asked him for his musical advice.

At my suggestion, Ellen would narrate Copland's *Lincoln Portrait*. She had done it with Arthur on a few occasions, and she knew it well. Before she appeared on the stage that night, I told the huge audience, "For fifty years there has been a Fiedler on this stage, and tonight is no exception."

Arthur listened to it on the radio, and when we returned to his house after the concert, he was still propped up in bed.

"How was it?" I asked.

"Fine," he said, "but the bass drum was too loud."

Arthur was in his eighty-fifth year when he died — a young age for a venerable conductor when one considers the longevity of Stokowski, Toscanini, Monteux, and many others, all of whom lived well into their late eighties and early nineties. As Arthur had indicated in his speech to the Stritch medical school audience in Chicago, some cardiologists believe there is a correlation between the vigorous physical exercise required to conduct and the corresponding benefit to the heart muscle. It has been reliably estimated that the physical effort expended by a conductor during one concert is equivalent to playing six sets of tennis.

Arthur was convinced his heart became stronger after each attack. After one coronary, Dr. Levine came backstage during intermission and ordered Arthur to remove his shirt. Upon examining the maestro, Levine shook his head with disbelief. "Whatever you're doing," he sighed, "keep it up."

Emily Weingarth accredited Arthur's many years of good health to alcohol. "He was pickled and preserved inside, which was what kept him alive."

During Arthur's last months and days of illness he remained in charge of his own affairs — the master of himself and his household. The morning he died, July 10, 1979, Ellen found him on the floor beside his bed. He had been sitting at his desk, checkbook open, endeavoring to put things in order. Evidently, he was trying to get back into bed when he slumped to the floor, dying peacefully. His left fist was clenched tightly shut. His right hand was raised as though he was still conducting. And perhaps he still is. As Morton Gould said to Yummie, "Don't grieve too much. He's probably up in heaven driving God crazy!"

Arthur's death inspired reminiscences and accolades from many corners. Emanuel Borok, concertmaster for the Pops, said:

"There is no such thing as Pops in Russia. It was absolutely a new thing to me when I came five years ago, and Fiedler knew that. Pops had such an enormous repertory. A large part of it was unknown to me, especially the American stuff. Fiedler was worried how I would do it. Then, one night on tour in Ames, Iowa, I was in a good mood. I'd had dinner and a few drinks. We were performing the *Fiddler on the Roof* collections. I felt the violin solo wasn't written right. It wasn't Jewish enough. So I played it the way I thought it should sound, added a few grace notes. Everybody in the orchestra laughed. And Fiedler laughed, too. After that, he never gave me any trouble, always let me do things my way."

Michael Steinberg, director of publications for the Boston Symphony Orchestra, noted:

"There was at one time a real serious musician (in him), and that's the part of him that everyone lost sight of, including himself. And I don't think he was ever completely at peace with himself because of that. He set very much store by such things as the Fiedler Sinfonietta (which recorded Handel organ concertos with E. Power Biggs), or the fact that, at one time, the Pops had performed more Mozart piano concertos than the Boston Symphony."

*   *   *

Arthur's death on July 10, 1979, brought to an end an unprecedented era in the history of the Boston Pops and of music in America. To an entire generation, the Pops was Arthur Fiedler. In the minds of countless thousands, the Pops began with Arthur Fiedler — no matter that he was actually the eighteenth conductor. To most people, Arthur was the *only* conductor.

For a few years before Arthur's death, there had been a number of guest conductors — Erich Kunzel, John Covelli, Mitch Miller, Morton Gould, John Green, Newton Wayland, Henry Mancini, John Lanchberry, Norman Leyden, and John Williams — all of whom had great success. All were being considered as successors to Arthur Fiedler. Some of them would have taken the job if offered, others would not. It was simply a stroke of good fortune and André Previn's intervention on our behalf that John Williams was not only interested, but available. Here was a man of solid musical background, trained in the classics, but experienced and knowledgeable in the American popular milieu. He was a composer of highly successful motion picture music, had won three Academy Awards, and his name was known to the public for his music for *Star Wars, The Empire Strikes Back,* and many other films.

When his appointment was announced on the front pages of newspapers throughout the country, I realized for the first time the importance of the Boston Pops on the American scene — something even Arthur had never imagined.

"If the transition had happened twenty years ago," I told Richard Dyer of the Boston *Globe,* "I would have expected to have the chance to follow Arthur. But at my age now, I didn't expect to get it, though I knew I was one of those being considered.

"There is something in the psychology of symphony orchestras about being an assistant — it practically never happens that they go on to the bigger job. It happens all the time in the business world, but practically never in an orchestra. I think that getting John Williams was a stroke of genius. Not only a fine musician, he is warm and sensitive, a person of great decency, and very modest; I don't know if I have ever met a more humble conductor. He is a dear man, and I feel very good about working with him."

As the Pops goes into a new era under its new conductor there will be the inevitable comparisons between what was the old and what will be the new. But perhaps there will not be that great a change. When Arthur became conductor some fifty years ago, he wisely continued the established format of mixing the classics with the popular standards of the day. The three-part program formula was retained, and it seems John Williams will continue that tradition. I believe he realizes tradition is an integral part of the Boston culture. Yet, I am convinced, he will also bring to the Pops some of his own personality. He has stated that a tune by Jerome Kern, Sigmund Romberg, or George Gershwin can be, in its own way, as hauntingly beautiful as a Schubert melody. Like Arthur Fiedler, John Williams is a musical anti-snob. He is also a fine conductor who knows how to bring out the best in his musicians. Williams realizes the enormous task ahead — that of following in the footsteps of a champion. In a way, John Williams's job is more difficult than the one Arthur accepted when he took over the Pops podium a half-century ago. At that time, the reputation of the Pops was at a low ebb and, although Arthur could have failed, the Pops had nowhere to go but up. Williams is taking over an orchestra at the height of its popularity. However, all indications are that John Williams will bring the Boston Pops to even greater heights. Times change, tastes change, and music changes. The Pops will change with it.

Immediately after Arthur's death, the Boston Symphony Orchestra Trustees voted to name the planned west wing of Symphony Hall the Arthur Fiedler Memorial Wing. They also voted to develop the Arthur Fiedler Boston Pops Fund to finance Esplanade Concerts and Pops activities.

"This will be a tangible and enduring memorial to an extraordinary man," said Talcott M. Banks, Chairman of the Board.

Arthur was cremated, as he requested, but he was not laid to rest in the manner he desired.

"May God forgive me," Ellen said. "He lies in the Bottomley plot in the cemetery next to where I shall be buried some day."

Coda

JULY 24, 1979 — HARVARD MEMORIAL CHURCH —
The eulogy continued with my words. What do I think
of this man now, after recalling all of these details, remembering
many of the incidents — humorous, embarrassing, and often
spiteful? I suppose I still feel much the same as I did when I
said of him at the memorial service at Harvard:

We can only hope that he would forgive us for what we say and
do here today in his honor, for Arthur was suspicious of flattery and
he was always embarrassed by praise. He was an unpretentious man
who had a job to do, and he did it as well as he could. He was a
man of complete self-effacement, lack of vanity, and almost maniacal
dedication to his work, to the music he played, and to the public
he served. Each concert was, for him, the first, and he took nothing
for granted. His whole life, his very religion was music, and his was
a no-nonsense approach to his craft. He never even stopped to think
of who he was and, when I once told him he didn't even know
he was Arthur Fiedler, he looked at me quizzically and said, "Nonsense."

Arthur Fiedler became during his lifetime a legend and a symbol.
A symbol for the common man, a symbol which made it possible
for millions of people to identify themselves with the beauty, the
joy, the fun of music, thus enhancing the quality of their lives. He

took music out of its ivory tower and brought it to the people, and he did it with dignity and mutual respect. Arthur Fiedler was good for the Boston Symphony, he was good for the city of Boston, he was good for the thousands of musicians who shared in his glory, he was good for me, and he was good for the world. All of these things I could not say during his lifetime and I can well imagine him looking down upon me now, wagging his finger and saying, "Harry, you could have at least started in the middle." To his family may I suggest, as he would, that you wipe away your tears and rejoice that he has left you and us a legacy and a tradition. We can do his memory no greater honor and ourselves no greater service than by continuing his tradition.

Epilogue

BY JOHN WILLIAMS

M Y RELATIONSHIP WITH ARTHUR FIEDLER was conducted entirely on the telephone. On a few occasions he rang me in California to ask if he could use some of my film music for his concerts, and the last time I spoke with him he asked if I would be available to write a piece for his Fiftieth Anniversary concert. Alas, at the time I was busy doing film work, with the result that I never had the pleasure of meeting this remarkable gentleman.

Of course, I had seen and heard him conduct many times on television and had always appreciated his ability to communicate so beautifully, with what had grown to be a massive and loving audience. I knew that he had built and maintained an extraordinary musical institution, but I had no conception of the enormity of what he did until I was invited to conduct in Boston. When I arrived there, I learned that the Pops played not two times each week, as I had thought, but performed six concerts a week, each week, for the duration of the Pops season.

Considering that Arthur Fiedler maintained this pace for fifty seasons, this is a staggering achievement. This amount of conducting, on a purely physical level, would be equivalent, say, to pitching five or six major league baseball games each week . . .

a daunting workload even for a person several decades younger than Fiedler. One was instantly aware that this was a man of extraordinary energy, who possessed a breadth of knowledge in the field of light music repertoire that was unique.

And his success was truly unique. As far as I know, he was the only person in the history of music who held a major conducting post for fifty years. Not even Johann Strauss, the waltz king, in his great days in Vienna, could have claimed to have had a greater success with his concerts, both musically and as a social event, than Arthur Fiedler had in Boston. Another fascinating aspect of this success is the fact that Fiedler was one of those rare human beings fortunate enough to be more attractive and more effective with each passing year. His popularity never ceased to grow, and I personally think that the achievement made in his later years is an inspiring part of his story.

Bearing all of this in mind, you can imagine the trepidation with which I arrived in Boston to start my first series of concerts as successor to this great man. I was the "new boy in town," being scrutinized by Arthur Fiedler's loving audience. I needn't have worried — everyone, the orchestra, management, and the Boston public made me feel instantly welcome. One could immediately sense the overriding sentiment of all present. There was an undying affection for the institution that he served so well and so long. Added to this were the wishes of everyone for the brightest possible future of the Pops.

Truly, the Pops is a great institution. It has been dedicated to presenting the best of the light music repertory along with the most appealing and worthy pieces of popular music. It has proudly presented our own American popular music, which unquestionably has been one of our greatest cultural achievements. American jazz and popular music are loved and imitated all over the world and for a long time have been some of our most important exports. The Pops and other institutions like it can serve a most valuable function in the preservation and presentation of this music, as future generations learn to know and want to hear Gershwin, Kern, Porter, Ellington, and all the rest.

But this is not to suggest that the Pops should represent an "atavistic movement" or perform a museumlike function. This would not be enough. The Pops can make a great contribution toward an exciting future, but only with the acceptance of a certain amount of change can we achieve that healthy continuity that will carry us from the brilliant past that the Pops enjoyed to the kind of future that it deserves. We must encourage new pieces to be written, and along with the performances of these things, we must continue to search for the best new composing and performing talents among our young people.

At the present time, Harry Ellis Dickson and I are the custodians of Arthur Fiedler's great legacy, and as we near the end of the century, we can look forward to a bright future, a future in which we present the best of the new and preserve the best of what we have inherited from the past. This is our challenge and our joy, as we continue in the great tradition of the "Boston Pops."